Dear Friend,

I'm pleased to send you this copy of *U-Turns: Reversing the Consequences in Your Life* by my friend Tony Evans. Tony is the founder and president of The Urban Alternative. He's also a pastor, bestselling author, and frequent speaker at the Billy Graham Training Center at The Cove.

Our decisions in life matter, and unfortunately we all have some we later regret. When our choices don't line up with God's Word, the consequences are dire. In this book, Tony offers Biblically based steps you can take to reverse course and get back on the path God has established for us. For the Christian, that U-turn is called repentance. I pray that this book will be an encouragement to you so that "*times of refreshing may come from the presence of the Lord*" (Acts 3:20, ESV).

For more than 70 years, God has used the Billy Graham Evangelistic Association (BGEA) and friends like you to reach people all over the world with the Gospel. I'm so thankful for the ways He has worked—and what He will do in the years ahead.

If you represent one of the lives the Lord has touched, we would love to hear from you. Your story has the power to impact the lives of so many others. May God richly bless you.

Sincerely,

Franklin Graham
President & CEO

If you would like to know more about our ministry, please contact us:

IN THE U.S.:
Billy Graham Evangelistic Association
1 Billy Graham Parkway
Charlotte, NC 28201-0001
BillyGraham.org
info@bgea.org
Toll-free: 1-877-247-2426

IN CANADA:
Billy Graham Evangelistic
    Association of Canada
20 Hopewell Way NE
Calgary, AB T3J 5H5
BillyGraham.ca
Toll-free: 1-888-393-0003

TONY EVANS

U-Turns

Reversing the Consequences in Your Life

PUBLISHING GROUP

NASHVILLE, TENNESSEE

This *Billy Graham Library Selection* special edition is published with permission from B&H Publishing Group.

©2020 by Tony Evans
All rights reserved.
Printed in the United States of America

978-1-4627-9061-6
ISBN: 978-1-593-28703-0 (BGEA edition)

Dewey Decimal Classification: 248.84
Subject Heading: CHRISTIAN LIFE / DISCIPLESHIP / GOD—WILL

Unless otherwise noted, all Scripture quotations are taken from the Christian Standard Bible®, copyright © 2017 by Holman Bible Publishers. Used by permission. Christian Standard Bible® and CSB® are federally registered trademarks of Holman Bible Publishers.

Also used: New American Standard Bible (NASB), copyright © 1960, 1962, 1963, 1968, 1971, 1972, 1973, 1975, 1977, 1995 by The Lockman Foundation.

Also used: English Standard Version (ESV). Text Edition: 2016. Copyright © 2001 by Crossway Bibles, a publishing ministry of Good News Publishers.

Also used: New Life Version (NLV), copyright © 1969, 2003 by Barbour Publishing, Inc.

Also used: New King James Version (NKJV), copyright © 1982 by Thomas Nelson. Used by permission. All rights reserved.

Cover design by Molly von Borstel, FaceOut Studio. Arrow icon from Annisa Aulia Istiqomah/shutterstock. Author photo © Joshua Farris.

It is the Publisher's goal to minimize disruption caused by technical errors or invalid websites. While all links are active at the time of publication, because of the dynamic nature of the internet, some web addresses or links contained in this book may have changed and may no longer be valid. B&H Publishing Group bears no responsibility for the continuity or content of the external site, nor for that of subsequent links. Contact the external site for answers to questions regarding its content.

1 2 3 4 5 6 • 24 23 22 21 20

Contents

Acknowledgments

I would like to thank LifeWay Christian Resources and B&H Publishing for their long-standing relationship in publishing, events, and film. It is always a joy to get to work on a project with such Spirit-led servants of the King. I especially want to thank Bill Craig for shepherding this relationship over the years. I also want to thank Taylor Combs and Kim Stanford for their work in reviewing and laying out this manuscript. Lastly, I want to thank Heather Hair for her continued dedication to my written library through her collaboration on this manuscript.

CHAPTER ONE

You Are Free to Choose Your Direction

Many years ago, out in the country, there lived a young boy in a home without plumbing. His family's house sat on a parcel of land far removed from much of civilization. As can be expected, an outhouse had been constructed some distance from the home. It sat close to a steep ledge that overlooked a creek.

This young boy hated the fact that, regardless of the weather, he had to walk quite a distance to go use the outhouse. Whether night or day, he had to leave the comfort of his home and make the long trek. On one occasion, this little boy's frustration got the best of him and, in a moment of sheer emotion, he shoved the rickety outhouse off of the ledge and into the creek down below.

Later that day, his father approached him with a very grave look on his face. "Son?" he asked.

"Yes, Daddy?" the boy replied, sheepishly.

"Did you push the outhouse off of the ledge and into the creek?"

The son hung his head in shame and said, "Yes, sir, Daddy. I did it."

The father then began to tell him what his punishment would be, only to be interrupted by his son. "But Daddy," he said, trying to get out of his impending punishment, "wait a minute. I learned that when George Washington's father asked him if he cut down the cherry tree, that he told the truth and admitted he did it. And then his father didn't punish him." The boy paused, searching for his father's response on his face. Then he continued when there was none, "I told the truth too. I shouldn't be punished either."

To which his father replied, "Yeah, but George Washington's father wasn't *in* the cherry tree when George chopped it down!"

This humorous story reminds us on a more profound note that decisions really do matter.

When God created humanity, He gave us a will with a capacity to choose. We all have the freedom to make our own choices. Within God's sovereign boundaries, He has established a field of play that allows for our decisions. Like a football field that has lines that do not move, teams are allowed to call their own plays within the sovereign lines and boundaries. The plays they call, along with their skillful execution of those plays, by and large determine the outcome of their game.

In creation, God sits sovereignly over our field of play. He has established certain lines that are nonnegotiable. He is King. He sets the boundaries in His realm. Yet within those lines, He has also chosen to give us freedom. He has given us choice. He has created us with the uniquely human characteristic known as free will.

Decisions really do matter.

For example, He told Adam and Eve in the garden, "You are free to eat from any tree of the garden, but you must not eat from the tree of the knowledge of good and evil, for on the day you eat from it, you will certainly die" (Gen. 2:16–17). Bottom line: God told Adam and Eve that they could choose. He gave them options. He even told them about the consequence if they chose poorly. But then He removed His hands of control on their conscience and allowed them to make the decision.

In giving humanity choice, evil became an option. God never forced evil into the human equation; rather, He allowed it. However, humanity actualizes it when we choose anything that goes against the sovereign and preferred will of God's rule.

You and I have been given freedom. And while that truth delights us, what many often forget is that with freedom comes responsibility. Yes, we have the freedom to choose for God or to choose against God. Yet while we have full ability to make our own choices in this life we've been given, we do not get to choose the consequences. Those have been predetermined by God. Just as God told Adam and Eve that if they chose to eat from the forbidden tree, they would "certainly die," God has consequences established within His rules that will play out if or when we choose against Him.

The freedom to choose is not the freedom to determine the outcomes of those choices. That is a very critical point to understand, because oftentimes when we find ourselves searching for a U-turn or hoping for a reversal or calling on God to deliver us, we forget that it was our own choices that got us lost to begin with. And when we forget that, we also forget to come before the Lord in a spirit of humility rather than entitlement. Yes, He is a good God. No, He is not obligated to make everything good in your life. Romans 8:28 says that God will work all things together for good to those who love Him and are called to His purposes. It doesn't say that all things will be, or will feel, good as they happen.

You may have picked up this book because you are tired of harvesting bitter and failed crops from wrong choices. You may have grabbed this book because you wanted a solution to your life's struggles. And if that's you, then this is the right book. That is my aim in ministering to you through these paragraphs, pages, and points. But what I won't do is give you a solution softened from the blows of God's truth. I won't do that because that is no solution at all. Your U-turn takes place precisely at the signposts of His truth, and nowhere else.

In the passage I've chosen to begin this book, Moses has reached his golden years and is delivering one of his final sermons. The children of Israel are about to cross over into the Promised Land; yet before they cross over, Moses wants to talk to them about their freedom to choose. He wants to remind them of the lessons he's learned the hard way, along with those who wandered aimlessly in the wilderness before them. Moses wants to send them forward on good footing so that they can experience all the blessings God has for them. He wants to remind them of the importance of living their lives according to the covenant.

Several times in his speech to his people, Moses uses this term: *covenant*. In fact, his entire talk is even introduced to us in Scripture with a double emphasis on the covenant. We read in Deuteronomy 29:

> These are the words of the covenant that the LORD commanded Moses to make with the Israelites in the land of Moab, in addition to the covenant he had made with them at Horeb. (v. 1)

> Therefore, observe the words of this covenant and follow them, so that you will succeed in everything you do. (v. 9)

... that you may enter into the covenant of the Lord your God, which he is making with you today, so that you may enter into his oath. (v. 12)

I am making this covenant and this oath not only with you, but also with those who are standing here with us today in the presence of the Lord our God and with those who are not here today. (vv. 14–15)

The Lord will . . . single him out for harm from all the tribes of Israel, according to all the curses of the covenant written in this book of the law. (vv. 20–21)

Then people will answer, "It is because they abandoned the covenant of the Lord, the God of their ancestors, which he had made with them when he brought them out of the land of Egypt." (v. 25)

A covenant is a divinely ordained and authorized relational bond. It is an official arrangement through which God reveals Himself. A covenant is not a casual discussion. When a man and woman get married, they become bound covenantally. That means a legal action has occurred, not merely a get-together or event. The covenant indicates that, by law, the two are now related as husband and wife.

Israel was God's covenant people. They belonged to Him in an officially arranged way. That's why in Deuteronomy 30:19, the language Moses uses resembles language you would hear in a court of law. He says, "I call heaven and earth as witnesses against you today." He speaks of witnesses. He speaks of a formal setting. The covenant between God and His people as they entered into the Promised Land provided the boundaries within which they were to operate. On one hand, when they chose to abide by the covenant, they would receive the benefits of the covenant, such as God's covering. But when they chose not to abide by the covenant, they would receive the curses of the covenant—otherwise known as consequences.

I often compare a covenant to an umbrella. An umbrella doesn't stop the rain from coming down, but when you are underneath the covering of the umbrella, it stops the rain from reaching you. Divine covering is a benefit of a covenant. But along with the benefits, there are also negative repercussions. Moses spoke of these as the blessings and the curses. When you read about the Mosaic covenant in Deuteronomy 28 and 29, you come to identify these blessings and curses and how they relate to various aspects of life. Whether it has to do with economics, fruitfulness, family stability, length of days, or business success and failure, the outcomes of individuals' choices come tied to those choices.

Now, you may be thinking about right now that this is all well and good for the Old Testament. You might be dismissing this opening chapter so far because I'm writing about the Israelites and the law of Moses. It's true that we are not under the law of Moses, but under the law of Christ. That's why I want to remind you in

Hebrews 7:22, the author tells us clearly that we are still under a covenant. He uses the exact same word. We read, "Because of this oath, Jesus has also become the guarantee of a better covenant." And while it might be a "better covenant," it is still a covenant. It still comes with choices, as well as consequences for those choices. Thus, when you or I choose to operate outside of the covenantal relationship and rule of the Lord Jesus Christ over our lives, we willingly pursue the negative consequences of our rebellion.

Jesus summed up His relational rule succinctly in His response to a lawyer seeking to test Him. He said,

> When the Pharisees heard that [Jesus] had silenced the Sadducees, they came together. And one of them, an expert in the law, asked a question to test him: "Teacher, which command in the law is the greatest?"
>
> He said to him, "'Love the Lord your God with all your heart, with all your soul, and with all your mind.' This is the greatest and most important command. The second is like it: 'Love your neighbor as yourself.' All the Law and the Prophets depend on these two commands." (Matt. 22:34–40)

Love. This one word lays the foundation of the entirety of the Law as well as the teaching of the Prophets. We are to love God and love others. Anything that we choose to do outside of that one word is rebellion against the new covenant. And, as we will learn throughout our time together in this book, rebellion produces consequences.

The choice is ours. And with our choices come either blessings or curses. God made it clear that we live underneath a governing covenant in both the Old Testament and the New.

If you have a child who tells you that they are not going to do what you say, all the while living underneath your authority in your home, that child has made a choice against your rule and relationship. Consequently, you will allow that child to suffer the results of that choice—whether it be punishment from you or loss of privileges. Now, keep in mind, your child's disobedience in no way severs his or her biological or legal relationship with you. He or she is still your child, and you still love him or her as your child. Likewise, our sin does not sever our relationship with God; if we have truly been born again, trusting in the sacrifice of Jesus Christ for the forgiveness of our sins, nothing can separate us from Him or keep us from entering heaven. But what your child's disobedience does bring upon them is a loss in the immediate benefit from you.

> *We are to love God and love others. Anything that we choose to do outside of that one word is rebellion against the new covenant.*

Similarly, when you or I choose to live in disobedience to Christ's rule of love toward God and others, we have removed ourselves from the flow of the blessings of God's covenant in many ways. When Moses addressed the Israelites, he told them they had a choice. He said, "I call heaven and earth as witnesses against you today that I have set before you life and death, blessing and curse" (Deut. 30:19a).

They could choose life. Or, they could choose death. There were no in-between choices. A non-choice was still a choice, because it was not a choice for life. Not to choose is to choose.

Moses laid it all out on the table for them, just as it is laid out for us today under the commandment of love. We have two options: to love, or not to love. Everything relates to our relationship to this new covenant of Christ just as everything related to the Israelites' relationship with the covenant Moses set before them.

What far too many Christians fail to understand is that, because they insist on living out of alignment underneath God, they choose to forfeit the abundant life Jesus said He came to give. You can't have both. Jesus said, "I have come so that they may have life and have it in abundance" (John 10:10). But, as with Moses and the Israelites, this life comes tied to the covenantal alignment underneath God's relational rule.

Moses encouraged the Israelites to choose life. He painted a word picture of what choosing life means when he told them:

"Choose life so that you and your descendants may live, love the LORD your God, obey him, and remain faithful to him. For he is your life, and he will prolong your days as you live in the land the LORD swore to give to your ancestors Abraham, Isaac, and Jacob." (Deut. 30:19b–20)

To choose life meant to love God, obey His voice, and remain faithful to Him. In doing so, they were to experience life and prolong their days in the land God gave them. To choose life under Christ's rule remains vastly the same: to love God, obey His voice, hold fast to Him, and to love others. In doing so, we experience the abundant life Jesus has promised.

Now, He didn't say we will experience a problem-free life, but rather that we will have fulfillment in the living. We will have peace. As Jesus said, "I have told you these things so that in me you may have peace. You will have suffering in this world. Be courageous! I have conquered the world" (John 16:33). This life has troubles. It has struggles. It comes with disappointments, heartache, and grief. But in the midst of all that and more, Jesus promises that when we choose life through aligning under His covenantal rule, we get peace. Peace isn't the absence of pain; it is the presence of Jesus to carry you through.

I know firsthand the power of peace. When the walls of loss and uncertainty cave in around me, I know what it means to say the name of Jesus and be filled with His peace. It's that peace that gets you through the days you cannot get through on your own. But peace comes through choosing to align your heart, mind, and actions under the rule of God. When you are out of alignment, you have no legal claim to His peace.

One day I had gotten in my car to drive to the church. I pushed the garage door opener, but nothing happened. Needing to get to a meeting, I decided to call a repairman. The first thing he asked me to do was walk over to the garage door and check to see if the canisters at the bottom were facing each other, or if one had gotten knocked to face another direction. This is because when the two canisters fail to align with each other, the signal does not connect, and the garage door will not raise. As soon as I turned the one canister which had gotten knocked out of alignment back toward the other canister, my garage door opener worked just fine. I was free to leave, all because of this powerful thing called *alignment*.

The garage door was too heavy for me to open on my own. It was too difficult for me to force up. But a simple adjustment in alignment did the trick. Similarly, believers who refuse to align to divine rule in their lives face closed doors, blocked destinies, and trapped dreams. It's all about alignment. You cannot ask God for divine favor while simultaneously making choices that go against His revealed will. That's a contradictory request due to the nature of a covenant. Remember, a covenant is a divinely created relational bond that carries with it both blessings and consequences.

> *Believers who refuse to align to divine rule in their lives face closed doors, blocked destinies, and trapped dreams.*

Moses made it clear what the consequences would be if the Israelites did not choose life. He said in Deuteronomy 30:17–18:

"But if your heart turns away and you do not listen and you are led astray to bow in worship to other gods and serve them, I tell you today that you will certainly perish

12

and will not prolong your days in the land you are entering to possess across the Jordan."

They would perish. Their dreams would perish. Their plans would perish. Their hopes would perish. All because they chose to be led astray and worship other gods.

We may not have wooden idols in our culture today, or statues to bow down to, but we do have other gods whom far too many of us serve on a regular basis. People have chosen race over God, culture over God, class over God, gender over God, possessions and entertainment over God, and so much more. We keep making all these choices and wonder why things are so chaotic, not only in the world but also in the church. It's because we keep choosing idols over God's revealed rule.

How do you know when you've chosen an idol? An idol is any unauthorized person, place, thing, or thought that you look to in order to determine your decisions. Whomever, or whatever, influences you to the degree of making the final decision in your life is an idol. If it is not the true, living God and His Word, it is an idol.

You serve what you obey. You worship what you align underneath. If the entertainment industry sways your final decision about something, and it contradicts with God's rule, then that is your idol. Or if economics makes the final decision, or a friend, a relationship, even a spouse—all of these can be idols. After all, had Adam listened to God rather than Eve, he would not have also eaten the fruit. And we would be living a very different outcome today.

Any overruling of what God says on a subject in your life—whatever the person, place, thing, or thought is—at that moment and in that decision it becomes your god. It's your idol. And you have removed yourself from the covenantal covering of the umbrella. See, the covering no longer works when you choose an idol. When you choose financial profit over biblical principle, or you choose cultural norms over God's revealed rule—you are worshiping an idol. It's a lot more straightforward than most people like to think. Matthew 6:24 (NASB) states it this way: "No one can serve two masters; for either he will hate the one and love the other, or he will be devoted to one and despise the other. You cannot serve God and wealth." For personal application, you can substitute wealth in there for whatever it is that trumps God's rule in your life and draws you from an intimate relationship with Him. For example:

You cannot serve God and popular opinion.

You cannot serve God and people-pleasing.

You cannot serve God and dishonesty.

You cannot serve God and immorality.

You cannot serve God and pride.

You cannot serve God and secularism.

You cannot serve God and bitterness.

You cannot serve God and yourself.

You have to choose; what's more: you get to choose. And with those choices come consequences: blessings or curses. Essentially, you get to choose if you experience blessings or curses.

When you think about it, that is a really good thing. God has given us the opportunity to choose whether we want to experience blessings or curses—favor or futility. It's up to us. It's up to you. You get to choose.

Moses described this choice as one between choosing "life and prosperity" or choosing "death and adversity" (Deut. 30:15). Keep in mind that biblical terms for life and death aren't always tied to physical life and death. There would be no one left on earth to read this book if each of us were to die physically whenever we rebelled against God. Nor would there be anyone to publish and print it. Spiritual life involves connection to God and all He supplies. Spiritual death means separation from God who leads to inner turmoil, adversity, futility, and discontentment.

Unfortunately, today, there are many people who are spiritually dead. Even in the church. As a result, their lives are full of the compounding impact of years of negative consequences for wrong choices. But the good news is that we live under the new covenant. We live under the sacrificial atonement of Jesus Christ. We can make a U-turn on any wrong road at any time and start choosing life.

This U-turn begins on an off-ramp named Repentance. It starts by acknowledging the choices, or pattern of choices, that you have aligned and made under any other influencer than God Himself. It starts in this spirit of humility that admits wrongdoing.

Then, it continues on an overpass called Grace. This is what God gives you as you are returning to the Lord. You move forward by aligning your choices under His rule, according to His commandment of love, while taking, heart the principles of His Word.

God's Word is not a collection of archaic sayings on dusty pages meant only to inspire you. No, God's Word is your very life. As Moses said when he was wrapping up his final speech to the Israelites just before they crossed into the Promised Land:

> "Take to heart all these words I am giving as a warning to you today, so that you may command your children to follow all the words of this law carefully. For they are not meaningless words to you but they are your life, and by them you will live long in the land you are crossing the Jordan to possess." (Deut. 32:46–47)

God's Word is not an idle word for you. Indeed, it is your life. And by aligning your life choices under His Word and pursuing an intimate relationship with Him, you will experience the abundant life Jesus has for you. You get to choose whether or not you want that. God is not going to force you to have the blessings He promises to those who seek Him. You get to choose life or death.

At a university nestled in the hills of the eastern part of our nation sat a wise, aged philosopher. This philosopher had a reputation far and wide for giving sensible answers to any question, no matter how hard. No one could stump him. Yet one day some clever students thought they had come up with a way to do just that. One of the students caught a small bird and carried it into the wise, old man as the other students gathered around. The students had discussed their plan before entering. They had determined to ask the philosopher if the bird was dead or alive. If the philosopher said the bird was dead, the student would then open his hands and allow the live bird to fly away. And if the philosopher said the bird was alive, the student would squeeze the bird until it died. Either way, the philosopher would at long last be proven wrong. The students thought they had him on this one.

Yet when the student posed the question to the philosopher, and after the murmuring of the other students watching came to a complete silence, the philosopher said nothing at all. Rather, the philosopher looked at the hands of the student holding the bird, and then he looked up at the student himself, then he looked back at the bird in his hands. The student couldn't wait to prove him wrong, so he asked him again, "Is the bird dead or alive?"

To which the philosopher calmly replied, "The answer is in your hands."

The steering wheel to your U-turn along life's journey is in your hands.

CHAPTER TWO

The Key to Your Reversal

When a person has a master key to a facility, they can unlock any door. All doors are subject to this one key. A person may have an individual key to their individual room, but someone with a master key can gain access into all the rooms.

The reason I bring this up is because a delicate subject such as reversing the consequences or outcomes of poor choices is a very broad topic. There exists as many variables of scenarios in the lives of people reading this book as there are people reading this book! Each one of you is dealing with a unique set of circumstances that may be totally different from another person who is also reading this book. I won't be able to address each particular situation directly, but what I can give you throughout our time together is a master key. What we will go over together are the biblical principles and truths that will unlock every door.

You are not an exception to this key. Your situation is not so far gone that this key will not work. There is hope and I'm here to give it to you.

Now, this book is a little different than many I write because it is going to look at specific types of strongholds or negative outcomes individually. We will get into those after these first two chapters. You can read them all, or you can pick and choose the types of struggles you are dealing with personally. There is wisdom to be found in all, so whether or not you face each particular difficulty yourself, you may want to read through them anyhow in order to glean the bits of truth that can apply to other areas of your life or that will help you help others in difficult circumstances.

That's how Scripture is laid out for us in many ways as well. None of us are trying to collapse a gigantic stone wall around a city, but Joshua's account of the Jericho walls tumbling down contains spiritual truths that we can apply to our lives today. Last I checked, none of us needs to be spit out of a belly of a whale, but Jonah's account sheds light on biblical principles in dealing with darkness and difficult times caused by disobedience.

The various categories or groups of negative outcomes we will be looking at together in showing ways to do a U-turn in your life may not be your particular category, but I would encourage you to read through them just as much as those that do. Why? Because truth has a way of transcending specifics in order to take root and bear fruit in your soul.

Yet as we start our time together, I want us to look at one thing that applies to everything directly. This is what I call the master key. This one key will address the masses of scenarios that present themselves in the great variety of individuals who read this book.

Simply stated, the master key for U-turning away from negative outcomes in your life brought on by poor choices is a lifestyle of repentance. I touched on this a bit in chapter 1, but it is so important that we are going to dive deeper in this chapter. The only master key that opens the door for the possibility of the reversal of negative life circumstances brought on by sin is repentance.

Now, before we go further, I want to explain that, by and large, the biblical principles we are looking at in this book have to do with the negative outcomes brought on by sin. Personal sin. There exists a variety of issues and struggles in life that torment or taunt individuals that have nothing to do with their own personal sin. The key to their reversal is often rooted in forgiveness. And I'll look at some of those, such as discrimination, later on. But the overwhelming majority of negative life outcomes is rooted in sinful

> *The master key for U-turning away from negative outcomes in your life brought on by poor choices is a lifestyle of repentance.*

life choices so, for the most part, that is what we'll be looking at in our time together.

Sin is rarely a topic you hear much about today. It doesn't fit into the seeker-sensitive, politically correct atmosphere of our current church climate. Sure, we'll mention a mistake or lapse in judgment here or there, but say something about sin and people might get offended. But I've preached and pastored long enough to know that if I were to fear people getting offended by me then I've picked the wrong profession. Truth offends sometimes—especially when it involves truth about sin.

Repentance is necessary because sin is real. Deny the existence of personal sin and you deny the only available solution to the self-inflicted problems and consequences you face. Redefine sin and you have also removed your ability to turn from the negative outcomes of it.

Sin can be defined as any violation of God's divine standard. There are sins of commission—these include the things you do in violation of God's rule, falling short of His standard. Romans 3:23 tells us, "For all have sinned and fall short of the glory of God." There are also sins of omission—these include the things you don't do but know to do (e.g., love, give, serve). We read about sins of omission in James 4:17 (NASB) where it says, "Therefore, to one who knows the right thing to do and does not do it, to him it is sin."

Keep in mind, the word the Bible uses to describe these things is not *mistake*. Nor is it *my bad*. The biblical word for violating God's rule in your life is *sin*. It's not a popular word. But whenever you violate, transgress, or ignore the standard of God in your thoughts, actions, and words—you are sinning. You are violating the nature of God Himself. Scripture describes God as perfect and righteous in all His ways. He is a perfect Being. In the same way that you don't like trash, refuse, or garbage, God doesn't like sin because it is the antithesis of His nature. God cannot have a relationship with sin while maintaining His holy integrity. That means sin must be addressed before negative outcomes or consequences can be addressed, since sin is what brings consequences (Hosea 14:1).

I realize this is counter to the popular notion that we can all do what we want whenever we want simply because we want to. And you can, actually. You have free will. But you can't do whatever you want free of consequences. And if you want to reverse negative consequences in your life due to sin, you will need to first address the sin.

As a pastor I have the opportunity to counsel many people. Frequently the root of the issue they are dealing with has to do with sin. Far too often I get a response that the person doesn't want to deal with his or her sin. Rather, they want God to change their consequences without them having to face, or remove, their sin. But it doesn't work that way. You cannot eliminate the odor of rotting food in your trash can without removing the rotting food and cleaning up after it. Sure, you may be able to mask the smell for a minute through some air freshener you spray, but the stench of the rotting food will dominate once again in just a short while.

In the same way that a doctor or nurse wants the surgical room sterile because bacteria will contaminate the process, God's holiness demands that we address and repent of our sin. Unfortunately today, many people are stuck traveling down the wrong road in life, wanting God to leave their sin alone but get rid of the problems in their life, which resulted from their sin! They want God to make them feel better, look better, be better without dealing with the cause of the issues to begin with. Sin is an affront to a holy God as it is a violation of His divine standard.

Death is the outcome of sin in Scripture. We read:

". . . but you must not eat from the tree of the knowledge of good and evil, for on the day you eat from it, you will certainly die." (Gen. 2:17)

For the wages of sin is death, but the gift of God is eternal life in Christ Jesus our Lord. (Rom. 6:23)

"Look, every life belongs to me. The life of the father is like the life of the son—both belong to me. The person who sins is the one who will die." (Ezek. 18:4)

Then after desire has conceived, it gives birth to sin, and when sin is fully grown, it gives birth to death. (James 1:15)

Israel, return to the LORD your God, for you have stumbled in your iniquity. (Hosea 14:1)

You can see from these verses, and many more if you do a quick search on sin in Scripture, that whenever you sin, you die. Again, that does not mean you drop dead physically every time you sin. As you recall from the last chapter, the biblical meaning of death does not exclusively refer to annihilation of personhood. It does not refer to the cessation of existence. In the Bible, death means a separation. When you or I sin, a separation takes place between us and God. Fellowship with God is distanced and ultimately lost due to sin. He must remove Himself from the presence of sin.

Now, for the Christian, that doesn't mean you lose your salvation. Salvation has been secured through the sacrificial death and resurrection of Jesus Christ. But living in unrepentant sin does mean your fellowship with God is hindered. It clouds our sense of closeness with God, calls into question our assurance of our salvation, and prevents fruit that otherwise would grow, benefitting us and others.

When Adam and Eve sinned, the human race inherited spiritual death, relational death, emotional death, economic death, physical death, and eternal death. Thus, these negative outcomes and consequences show up in your life.

Some people reading this book are more dead than others. Some separation is further than others. And some has gone on longer than others. But all separation can be addressed through repentance. Repentance is the master key for whatever scenario you face today that is a result of sin. It opens the door based on God's prerogative to reverse, limit, cancel, or give you the capacity to handle the negative consequences in your life.

Repentance can be defined as the internal resolve and determination to turn from sin. Repentance is God's way of sowing back together the rupture with Him. Once that rupture is rejoined, the potential for reversing negative consequences exists. Yet none of this can occur without the personal, internal resolve and determination to acknowledge sin, turn away from sin, and move toward God. When you seek to repair your relationship with God through this internal resolve to deal with your sin, you have set the stage for your U-turn.

When John the Baptist came on the scene to initiate Jesus' public ministry, he preached a message of repentance. We read in Matthew 3:2–3: "'Repent, because the kingdom of heaven has come near!' For he is the one spoken of through the prophet Isaiah, who said: 'A voice of one crying out in the wilderness: Prepare the way for the Lord; make his paths straight!'"

The concept of kingdom refers to the rule of God. Thus, if you want to see God rule your situation or overrule your consequences, you must first repent. If you don't bother to repent, don't bother to pray. Don't waste your time asking God to deliver you from negative consequences if you are unwilling to repent of what got you there in the first place. Repentance is the master key to reunite your relationship with God so that He then intervenes in the consequences as His prerogative. It involves a change of your mind with the view of reversing a direction in life.

For starters, repenting must include a recognition of sin. This is manifested by sincere confession. If you don't believe there is sin, then you don't need to repent of it. But to confess something is to acknowledge it exists. First John 1:9 tells us that repentance involves confession. It says, "If we confess our sins, he is faithful and righteous to forgive us our sins and to cleanse us from all unrighteousness." The Greek word for *confess* means to say in agreement. It refers to saying the same thing as the other. You must say about your sin what God says about your sin. And, as we saw earlier, God does not call sin "your bad." It's not a mistake or lapse in judgment. It's not an "oops." It is willful disobedience against the standard of a righteous and holy God. Plain and simple.

Unless and until you acknowledge and confess your willful disobedience against the standard of a holy God, you will not be on the path of making a U-turn from negative consequences caused by sin.

If God calls something sin, you and I ought not to call it a bad habit. When God says something is sin, it doesn't matter what your friends say it is. Oftentimes in today's culture, it doesn't even matter what your pastor says it is. Fear of losing congregants has silenced so many pastors from calling sin as it is: sin. You and I must confess sin as sin in order for God to address it and repair our relationship with Him. No, I don't think this type of teaching will make me popular. But popularity has never been my goal. Speaking the truth of God under His rule in my life has always been my goal.

Thus, the first thing you need to do to reverse negative outcomes in your life due to sin is to confess your sin to God.

Accompanying your confession of sin is what the Bible calls in 2 Corinthians 7:10–11 "godly sorrow" (NASB). Godly sorrow differs from being sorry you got caught. That, Paul says, is "worldly sorrow." Godly sorrow isn't just being upset about your consequences; it's recognizing you've hurt the heart of God. As David said in Psalm 51:4, "Against you—you alone—I have sinned . . ." Godly sorrow is the sorrow that leads to repentance. It involves remorse. Sorrow, for the sake of sorrow, won't be enough to get you turned around and on the right path.

Paul explains the difference between godly sorrow and worldly sorrow in 2 Corinthians 7:8–10 (NASB) when he says:

> For though I caused you sorrow by my letter, I do not regret it; though I did regret it—for I see that that letter caused you sorrow, though only for a while—I now rejoice, not that you were made sorrowful, but that you were made sorrowful to the point of repentance; for you were made sorrowful according to the will of God, so that you might not suffer loss in anything through us. For the sorrow that is according to the will of God produces a repentance without regret, leading to salvation, but the sorrow of the world produces death.

The two examples of Peter's sorrow and Judas's sorrow illustrate this profoundly. When Judas betrayed Jesus for thirty pieces of silver, the Bible tells us that he came to the point where he felt sorrow. But the sorrow he felt was not godly sorrow. As a result, the negative emotions and consequences he had become embroiled in led to him killing himself. We read:

> Then Judas, his betrayer, seeing that Jesus had been condemned, was full of remorse and returned the thirty pieces of silver to the chief priests and elders. "I have sinned by betraying innocent blood," he said.
>
> "What's that to us?" they said. "See to it yourself!" So he threw the silver into the temple and departed. Then he went and hanged himself. (Matt. 27:3–5)

Judas felt sorrow, no doubt. He regretted what he had done. But his was a worldly sorrow leading only to further death. Instead of turning away from his sin and toward God, he turned away from his sin and to himself. Luke later writes, "Now this man acquired a field with his unrighteous wages. He fell headfirst, his body burst open and his intestines spilled out" (Acts 1:18). He had added sin upon sin through personal blame and punishment, leaving himself (literally) empty.

On the contrary, when Peter sinned against Jesus, his sorrow was rooted in a godly repentance. We read how Peter responded in Luke 22:61–62 when he was confronted with his sin. It says:

> Then the Lord turned and looked at Peter. So Peter remembered the word of the Lord, how he had said to him,

"Before the rooster crows today, you will deny me three times." And he went outside and wept bitterly.

Peter and Judas had sinned against Jesus. Judas had betrayed Jesus, while Peter had denied him. In both accounts in Scripture we read how sadness was felt. And yet Judas sealed his legacy as a deceiver, liar, and betrayer, while Peter went on to create a legacy of leadership and love. How did these men wind up with such vastly different endings to their stories? The reasons can be found in the fine line that exists between worldly sorrow and the godly sorrow that leads to repentance.

Judas felt remorse, which includes that personal distress that bubbles up in the soul when guilt over personal choices or wrongs takes place. This personal distress dead-ends in self-reproach and shame. But Peter, on the other hand, repented. How do we know he repented? Is it because he "wept bitterly"? No. In fact, a person can weep bitterly when their sins have found them out and consequences abound. We know that Peter repented because repentance always involves a change in pursuit. It includes a change of direction. It is a U-turn from the sin itself.

Peter's sin that led him to deny Jesus was due to his fear of others and his need for self-preservation. We know that Peter pursued a different direction in his repentance because it was evidenced not long after when he ran to the tomb to see if Jesus was still there, even though Roman guards had been positioned at its opening to guard it. He ran toward the danger rather than away from it. We also know Peter's repentance produced a change of direction because when Jesus appeared on the seashore while Peter was fishing, as we read in John 21, Peter jumped into the water and swam directly toward Him. He couldn't even wait for the boat to dock.

What's more, following Jesus' ascension, Peter proudly proclaimed the message of Jesus Christ even at the risk to his own well-being. Multiple times he was imprisoned for doing so, only to be released and do it again. This man who had once cowered in fear denying Jesus now stood boldly proclaiming His name, at the risk of even losing his own life. We read of the fruits of Peter's repentance in Acts 5:

> After they brought them in, they had them stand before the Sanhedrin, and the high priest asked, "Didn't we strictly order you not to teach in this name? Look, you have filled Jerusalem with your teaching and are determined to make us guilty of this man's blood."
>
> Peter and the apostles replied, "We must obey God rather than people." (vv. 27–29)

Judas and Peter both acknowledged the sinfulness of their words and actions. Both men felt some level of sorrow. Yet only Peter repented. Repentance produces a change of mind about the sin, thus prompting a change in actions. Peter's repentance led to peace. Peter's response led to life. Peter's response created a U-turn which brought about what Matthew 3:8 says, ". . . fruit consistent with repentance."

Nobody has seen invisible fruit. Fruit is always something you can see. It comes in different shapes and sizes, but it is always visible. In other words, you know it's an apple tree because you see the apples. You know it's a pear tree because there are pears. You know it's an orange tree when you see some oranges. Similarly, you know you are truly repentant when you see the fruit of your repentance. You see the change of direction in your thinking, words, and actions. You are doing something that demonstrates a reversal.

You can't repent of extramarital sex and still keep having extramarital sex. You might feel bad about it. You might feel shame. But the action in and of itself has to change for it to be repentance. Neither can you repent of pornography and keep returning to internet porn sites. You have to set measures in place to change the behavior in keeping with the fruit of repentance, or it's not repentance. It may be sorrow, yes. It may even be regret. But, like Judas, worldly sorrow simply leads to more death through shame and self-defeating behavior.

Sure, some sins may have turned into addictive behavior, and stopping them cold turkey would be a challenge. But true repentance means you take the steps in the right direction toward stopping the sin. You confess to someone else. You ask for help. You create boundaries.

You know you are truly repentant when you see the fruit of your repentance.

You can always take a repentance step even if you have not yet reached the repentance goal. A repentance step is the fruit of a repentant heart. If there is no fruit in your life (an action step taken to reverse a sinful situation), then you have a right to question whether or not there was simply shame rather than spiritual repentance. Repentance always turns your spirit toward God and His relational rule in your life and produces a desire to reestablish fellowship with Him.

God wants to see you demonstrate repentance, not just talk about it. And while the sin may not disappear completely tomorrow, He wants to see you taking steps that reflect a return. Zechariah 1:3 reinforces this truth as we read: "So tell the people, 'This is what the LORD of Armies says, Return to me—this is the declaration of the LORD of Armies—and I will return to you, says the LORD of Armies.'"

Malachi also gives us this glimpse into God's heart on repentance and the action of returning. We read in Malachi 3:7: "'Since the days of your ancestors, you have turned from my statutes; you have not kept them. Return to me, and I will return to you,' says the LORD of Armies." Repentance involves returning to God. It is deeper than worldly sorrow. It involves more than emotion. Repentance is an action you take to move in the opposite direction. Repentance is not a button you push. It is a process that transforms your heart.

James explains what true repentance looks like when he writes,

> Therefore, submit to God. Resist the devil, and he will flee from you. Draw near to God, and he will draw near to you. Cleanse your hands, sinners, and purify your hearts, you double-minded. Be miserable and mourn and weep.

Let your laughter be turned to mourning and your joy to gloom. Humble yourselves before the Lord, and he will exalt you. (James 4:7–10)

This is not a fun process. If you really want to overcome Satan's dominance in your life and invite God's greater grace into the negative outcomes you face on a daily basis, it involves sorrow over your sin. It involves grieving over having grieved the heart of almighty God. Repentance is like a sergeant over a soldier saying:

About-face.

Reverse.

Shift your direction.

It is not about just words. Or, even just prayer. If you are still facing and fretting over the negative consequences sin has brought your way, I would encourage you to examine—or reexamine—if you have ever truly repented of the source of those problems: sin. Repentance is to be a lifestyle. It is a way to operate. It's not an event. Jesus didn't die for, "I'm sorry," or, "Oops, my bad." Jesus died to open the way for us to return in our pursuit of fellowship and intimacy with God. He died to offer us the ability and opportunity to repent.

If you want to witness God intervene in your financial circumstances, or your emotional upheavals, or relational and spiritual mayhem, you must start by using the master key called repentance. We all have to use this same key. It doesn't matter who we are, how big our platform is, how many social media followers we have, or how much we say (or sing) about loving God. This master key of repentance belongs to all of us. Our deliverance is in our repentance. Acts 3:19–21 puts it this way:

> Therefore repent and turn back, so that your sins may be wiped out, that seasons of refreshing may come from the presence of the Lord, and that he may send Jesus, who has been appointed for you as the Messiah. Heaven must receive him until the time of the restoration of all things, which God spoke about through his holy prophets from the beginning.

Your refreshment and release from the dogpiling of repercussions related to personal sin comes only through repentance. Repent. Return. Be refreshed. It is literally that simple. But, as we will see through the various biblical accounts of types of consequences and their reversals, simple can sometimes be hard. Why? Because we make it hard.

As we go through these different subjects, will you do me a favor? Will you highlight in your Bible or write on a piece of paper or make a note on your smart device this one passage from Acts 3? The secret is in the master key. Your release is in this truth. Your U-turn toward your destiny is in these words:

> *Therefore repent and turn back, so that your sins may be wiped out, that seasons of refreshing may come from the presence of the Lord.*

Underline them. Memorize them. Meditate on them. Apply them. Experience them.

Remember your deliverance is in your repentance (Isa. 1:18–20).

Here's to your U-turn. Your best is yet to come.

CHAPTER THREE

Reversing the Consequences of Idolatry

 We live in the era of the selfie. Everywhere you go, people are taking photos of themselves. If God were walking among us in human form at this time in history, though, He would not take a selfie. This is because one of the things God said to His people is that they should never make an image of the living God.

The Israelites were strictly told not to carve, create, build, or fashion anything that would stand in resemblance of God. The only selfie God ever took in all of history was Jesus Christ. Jesus is God's selfie. Other than Jesus, He told humanity not to even attempt it because we would mess it up. At best, our attempts at making an image of God would be like a bad photograph you get from one of those photo booth machines. They are a cheap reflection of the real thing, and usually not something you show to very many people at all. They often distort reality. And in the spiritual realm, any distortion of who God truly is becomes idolatry.

Now, don't skim past this chapter because you think that idolatry is for faraway cultures in long-ago times. We live in an idol-saturated society. Although sophisticated, idols are everywhere.

An idol is any person, place, thing, or thought that someone looks to as their source. It could be their source of emotional well-being, or their source of provision, power, identity, good health, or any number of things. This is idolatrous because God is the source of everything we need. As believers we are to love the Lord our God first. Anything that competes with that love, honor, reverence, and alignment is an idol.

> *In the spiritual realm, any distortion of who God truly is becomes idolatry.*

Idols come in all shapes and sizes in an effort to compete with God and draw us away from God. Idols have one overarching purpose: to replace God's rightful rule in your life. As King, God is to be the preeminent ruler in all that you think, say, and do. We have been put here on the earth to carry out His kingdom agenda. The kingdom agenda can be defined as the visible manifestation of the comprehensive rule of God over every area of life.

Satan uses idols to draw us away from this legitimate rule of God. Satan and his demons do so by bringing in competitive forces to steer us from the truth in order to devolve us over time, and to hijack our decision-making. Virtually everything wrong in our lives that continues to crumble, even though it may have started out looking and feeling very right, is wrong because it is an idol. Every misguided path you take has an idol out front like the proverbial carrot before the donkey.

In order to do a U-turn and get off the wrong path of idolatry, you must first and foremost recognize the sin of idolatry for what it is. It is a clever ploy by the Enemy to get you going in a damaging and fruitless direction. The biblical account of Manasseh gives us great insight into this strategy by Satan, so we are going to examine this account in this chapter.

In 2 Chronicles 33, we're told about this man named Manasseh. Now, Manasseh is about as evil as evil gets. You'll see that as we go on. But the reason I want to point that out to you right now is because far too many people feel that they are simply too far gone for a U-turn. But that's never the case. I don't care how bad you have been or are now—God can give you a way out. Manasseh is proof of that.

Manasseh became king when he was only twelve years old. He would go on to reign as king for fifty-five years. Now, to appreciate his life story, you need to understand that he was raised in a God-fearing home. He was raised right. A summary of his father Hezekiah can be found in 2 Chronicles 29. The second verse summarizes Hezekiah's leadership the best when it says, "He did what was right in the LORD's sight, just as his ancestor David had done."

Manasseh had every opportunity to experience and learn from godly leadership. He was raised by a father who loved God, served Him, and wanted those around him to love God and serve Him too. But godly parenting does not guarantee godly offspring. In 2 Chronicles 33:2 we read that Manasseh chose to go the opposite direction of his father. He drove down a very different path. It says, "He did what was evil in the LORD's sight, imitating the detestable practices of the nations that the LORD had dispossessed before the Israelites." Hezekiah was a godly man. Yet his son, Manasseh, went way off course.

Manasseh caved into the call of the culture. The passage tells us that the evil he committed was "imitating the detestable practices of the nations that the LORD had dispossessed." Manasseh got lured by those around him. He adopted the worldview of other nations. They are called "abominations" according to the New American Standard translation, but the majority of people in those days did not see them that way. They would have called them fun, exciting, freedom of expression, political-correctness, or any number of things. Manasseh became popular with those who were popular, so to speak.

No doubt if Instagram were a thing back then, his would have millions and millions of followers, as he posted pictures of himself in various poses wearing whatever the styles of the day might be.

You need to keep in mind that what the Bible calls "abominations," culture calls cool.

Manasseh got enticed and sold out. He incorporated the world-view of the society that surrounded him, rather than the godliness that had reared him. As such, verses 3–6 tell us what he did:

> He rebuilt the high places that his father Hezekiah had torn down and reestablished the altars for the Baals. He made Asherah poles, and he bowed in worship to all the stars in the sky and served them. He built altars in the LORD's temple, where the LORD had said, "Jerusalem is where my name will remain forever." He built altars to all the stars in the sky in both courtyards of the LORD's temple. He passed his sons through the fire in Ben Hinnom Valley. He practiced witchcraft, divination, and sorcery, and consulted mediums and spiritists. He did a huge amount of evil in the LORD's sight, angering him.

You name it, Manasseh did it. Sorcery—known today as the horoscope. Divination—palm-readers or psychics. Child sacrifice—abortion. Witchcraft—Satanism and spells. Manasseh brought the idols of the culture into the house of God, much like many believers continue to do today, just under different names.

In fact, the culture so influences the church in today's world that people are bringing all sorts of evil into the arena of what had been intended for good. And churches just go along with it in order to have enough money, entice big enough crowds, get notoriety, keep people happy, and stay popular. You know that the culture is in trouble when the pulpit and the pew are acquiescing to the demands of society.

Idols exist everywhere. They aren't just wood carvings. There are educational idols. Social idols. Relational idols. Entertainment idols. Sports idols. Gender idols. Cause idols. Economic idols. We advertise personalities and platforms today as if they are gods. People literally spend hours upon hours each day scrolling through pictures on Facebook, Instagram, Twitter, and the like—following fools. They are following crazy, indecent people who just so happen to look good or know how to edit a photo. And these same people who will spend hours every day looking at fools can't seem to find five minutes to spend with God or reading His Word.

To say that we are a nation of idolatry is an understatement. Yet the God of creation does not stand for competition. He has an exclusivity clause. He has a no-compete contract. Thus, whenever you bring in competition or idolatry against His rightful place in your life, you will be driving in the wrong direction. You will have made the almighty God your enemy. As Ezekiel 14:6 says, there is only one right direction when it comes to idols: "Therefore, say to the house of Israel, 'This is what the Lord GOD says: Repent and turn away from your idols; turn your faces away from all your detestable things.'"

But doing a U-turn away from the idols is not what Manasseh did. In fact, 2 Chronicles 33:9 tells us that Manasseh even sped up in the wrong direction he had taken. We read: "So Manasseh caused Judah and the inhabitants of Jerusalem to stray so that they did worse evil than the nations the LORD had destroyed before the Israelites." He did more than the pagans, sinners, heathens, and sorcerers. He became completely intertwined with the demonic forces at hand. That's what idolatry is.

Manasseh had gotten so far off track that God sought to reel him back in. First, he spoke to him. But Manasseh wouldn't listen. Then, after he chose not to listen, God got his attention another way. We read:

> The LORD spoke to Manasseh and his people, but they didn't listen. So he brought against them the military commanders of the king of Assyria. They captured Manasseh with hooks, bound him with bronze shackles, and took him to Babylon. When he was in distress, he sought the favor of the LORD his God and earnestly humbled himself before the God of his ancestors. (vv. 10–12)

God broke Manasseh. He created a situation in which Manasseh would have to listen to Him. He allowed others to put hooks in him, chain him, and take him away to Babylon. Sometimes God will create chaos in our lives to get our attention. If our ears have become too dull to listen, and our hearts too hard to even ask questions and seek Him, then God will allow disruption to draw us back to Him.

Pay attention to the way the passage is worded. It doesn't say that the Assyrians went and captured Manasseh. It says that "[the

LORD] brought against them the military commanders of the king of Assyria." God brought the enemy in to topple him. Even sinners have to do what God says. Even the devil is on a leash. When you or I witness the negative influence or oppression of evil, we should not be too quick to point fingers. Oftentimes, God is guiding the actions and activities of people in order to bring about the greater good for all.

Sometimes God will create chaos in our lives to get our attention.

Hebrews 12:6 tells us why God sometimes does what He does when life doesn't feel good or go according to our plans. It says, "For the Lord disciplines the one he loves and punishes every son he receives." God will not tolerate idols that compete for His glory. He's not seeking to be mean, but if you or I won't listen when He speaks, discipline often comes next. That's why it is always best to listen to the Lord and align your thoughts, words, and actions under His overarching rule.

Manasseh learned this the hard way. In his distress, he humbled himself and listened to God. At times, God has to drive us to our knees. This is exactly what He did with Manasseh. God stripped him of his independence. He broke him of his self-sufficiency. He had called for voluntary surrender, but when Manasseh refused to hear Him, God gave him a reason to look up. Sometimes humanity just needs a little help in humility.

In football, the biggest players have to get the lowest in order to make the play. The larger you are, the lower you had better bend. Similarly, you and I will most fully live out our destiny and purpose in life when we humble ourselves and go low. God gives grace to the humble but resists the proud (James 4:6). This isn't a random thought or assumption. Scripture is replete with this reality:

Though the LORD is exalted, he takes note of the humble;
but he knows the haughty from a distance. (Ps. 138:6)

He mocks those who mock, but gives grace to the humble.
(Prov. 3:34)

A person's pride will humble him, but a humble spirit will
gain honor. (Prov. 29:23)

"Whoever exalts himself will be humbled, and whoever
humbles himself will be exalted." (Matt. 23:12)

"He has toppled the mighty from their thrones and exalted
the lowly." (Luke 1:52)

God has not stuttered regarding how He views pride. There should be no ambiguity on how we interpret His Word on this subject and concerning this specific idol. Most people do not view independence or pride as an idol, but it is. In fact, it's one of the main idols we are tempted to serve. There are no exceptions—we have all bowed to this idol at one time or another. Sure, some may have bowed at different levels or to different degrees, but we have all worshiped the idol of self-sufficiency, independence, and pride.

Manasseh bowed to pride, and it led him down a path of destruction. It wasn't until God let him reach the end of himself that Manasseh realized just how wrong his choices had been. He humbled himself before the Lord because he was in distress. Distress will do that. God can make us so desperate that we wind up discovering He is the only One to bow before.

Numerous times throughout Scripture, God released people to the mercy of their own idols. He stepped aside and let them find out what the idol produced. Time and time again it produced the same exact thing: disaster. It isn't until you and I learn dependence upon the One, true God that we will experience the full expressions of our destinies.

You remember the Lone Ranger shows as a kid? Or maybe you watch them now on cable. The Lone Ranger saw a horse, but the horse was a wild stallion. The horse wouldn't let the Lone Ranger ride him. The Lone Ranger would climb on, but the horse would buck him off. But instead of giving up and walking away, the Lone Ranger would climb back on again. And, again, he'd get bucked right off. This went on time and time again until eventually the horse learned that the Lone Ranger wasn't about to stop. He was willing to climb on and get bucked off as many times as was necessary to break the horse of its independence. This is because the

Lone Ranger saw something in the wild stallion. He saw something special.

Guess what? God only breaks us because He sees something in us worth pursuing. Only when God breaks us of our independence in order for us to align ourselves under His direction will we be free to reach our potential. As long as we are independent, we will simply wander through life alone. Yet when we yield to the mighty hand of God over our hearts, He gives us the ability to do and accomplish so much more. For some of us, that breaking can come quickly. For others, it takes trial after trial after trial before we will look up in humility to God like Manasseh did.

When Manasseh humbled himself before God, God responded:

He prayed to him, and the LORD was receptive to his prayer.
He granted his request and brought him back to Jerusalem,
to his kingdom. So Manasseh came to know that the LORD
is God. (2 Chron. 33:13)

God did a U-turn in Manasseh's life. He turned his situation around. He brought him out of Babylon and back to Jerusalem. Once Manasseh realized that the diviners, astrologers, spiritists, and Satanists couldn't help him, he called out in repentance to the One true God. When he finally came to understand that his money, power,

> *God only breaks us because He sees something in us worth pursuing.*

prestige, and influence couldn't redeem him, he turned to the One who could. And God showed Manasseh both mercy and grace. God was moved by his cry for help. One attribute we don't always associate with God is His emotion. Though there is much mystery here, and though His emotion is different than human emotion, the Bible over and over again shows us a God who responds to us with a tender, loving heart. When Manasseh humbled himself, God responded. And He always responds to true repentance and humility.

Psalm 103:10 says, "He has not dealt with us as our sins deserve or repaid us according to our iniquities." We also see this side of God in Isaiah 59:1–2:

> Indeed, the LORD's arm is not too weak to save, and his ear
> is not too deaf to hear. But your iniquities are separating
> you from your God, and your sins have hidden his face
> from you so that he does not listen.

God stays far when our sins separate us from Him relationally. He stays far because He knows He is unwelcome in an arena of idols. But when you and I humble ourselves before Him, He comes near. Just as He did with Manasseh. God returned Manasseh to the very place where it all went wrong in the first place. He placed him in the heart of Jerusalem once again. He brought him all the way back and reinstalled him in the very position He had kicked him out of. That is both mercy and grace. God didn't kick him to the curb. He didn't tell him, "Yes, I forgive you, but you will spend the rest of your life unused and in exile." No, God brought him back and put him in the same position. God decided what level of restoration Manasseh would get. And He also decides what level you get. No, it might not look the same in every person's life, but God's restoration of us always reveals His grace and mercy.

The good news that we should take from this account in 2 Chronicles is that God can meet us in the darkest places of our lives and even in the furthest reaches of our disobedience and dishonor. Not only can He meet us, He can redeem us. He can redeem you. You are not too far gone for God to restore you. You have not driven down the wrong road for so long that there is no way back. Humble your heart before the Lord, turn away from the idols that have ensnared you, and He will meet you where you are. He will lift you up.

There is a man who lives in DeSoto, Texas, and he is a junkyard specialist. He majors in other people's junk. This man will go to junkyards around the state and find stuff that has been thrown away. He'll see something in it that other people cannot see, so he'll buy the junk for a few dollars and take it back to his garage. There, he'll turn the junk into a piece of contemporary art, selling it for thousands of dollars.

Yes, at one point it looked like junk. In fact, it was junk. But in the hands of a master, even junk can turn into art.

You are not too far gone for God to restore you.

Your situation and your path may look littered and junky. Your circumstances and choices may appear unredeemable. But the good news of this message is that when you put your life in the hands of the Master, He can make you the masterpiece He designed you to be all along. No matter how long you've been off track, God can restore you. No matter how far you've gone in the wrong direction, God can redirect you. No matter how unreachable you feel, God is near you. Manasseh was at the bottom of the pit, but God still reached in and brought him home.

Two small kids were visiting their grandparents. One of them was feeling mischievous, so he walked out to the pond with his slingshot and hit a duck with a stone. He hit the duck so hard, the duck died. The little boy was scared because he knew how much his grandma loved the ducks, so he tried to hide the dead duck and go inside like nothing had happened.

The problem for him was, his sister had seen everything. She promptly let him know what she saw as well. Now the boy felt more than just guilt, he felt fear. As soon as the grandma asked his sister to set the table for dinner, that fear began to dictate his choices. His sister promptly replied, "Joey wants to set the table, Grandma." She winked at Joey. Joey jumped to set the table.

When their grandpa asked the sister to help take the trash out to the curb, she just winked at Joey again. Joey hopped up and took the trash out to the curb. This went on for days. Not only was Joey doing his own chores, but he was also doing his sister's. He had become her slave out of fear.

When Joey couldn't take it any longer, he finally confessed that he killed the duck. His grandma replied, "I know you killed the duck, Joey. I saw you kill the duck. I just didn't say anything because I wanted to see how long you were going to let your sister hold you hostage."

God has seen everything you have done. He knows how long you've done it and how deep it is. No matter how long you keep your sin unconfessed, you're not hiding it from God. He knows. But He also wants to see how long you are going to let the devil hold you hostage out of fear. He wants to see how long you are going to allow Satan to control you, define you, and misdirect you. God stands ready to forgive you and grant you a U-turn in life, but it is up to you to come to Him in humility and honesty first. He's waiting for your repentance. He's near.

Wouldn't it be nice to have Him take you back to where you belong? He will if you will humble your heart and seek His hand of grace and mercy.

CHAPTER FOUR

Reversing the Consequences of Addiction

 Many of God's children are spiritual POWs. They exist as prisoners of war, trapped in a sin cycle that they have been unable to break.

Whether it is alcoholism, materialism, bitterness, envy, gluttony, personal-pity, pornography, drugs, gaming, profanity, social media, negative self-talk, rage, or resentment, emotionally or chemically driven addictions confine far too many people today. Well-meaning people and organizations in our culture have produced an entire addiction-recovery industry in order to assist people to get out of the vise grip that is holding them hostage.

Yet despite the plethora of ministries, church groups, focus groups, clinics, hospitals, camps, and support systems available to people today, a large number of individuals remain unreleased from the death grip of addiction-based sins. Praying hasn't freed them. Sheer will hasn't freed them. Attending church or setting resolutions hasn't freed them. Thus, day after day there continues to be millions of those hearts, minds, and souls stuck in a self-defeating cycle of addictive behavior.

The biblical term for what we know today as addiction is *stronghold*. The word *stronghold* is used because it refers to both the physical and spiritual nature of the addiction. An addiction—or more accurately, a spiritual stronghold—is an entrenched pattern of negative thoughts and actions that we believe; and we function as though it is unchangeable even though it is against the will of God. It is a sin that has become a slave-master that rules our thoughts, decisions, and actions.

Far too many people simply seek to fix the physical and emotional aspect of an addiction without addressing the spiritual nature of it as well. Don't get me wrong—the physical and emotional aspects do need to be addressed, and there are professionals who can help in these areas. But if it is divorced from the spiritual component, this leads to failure and entrapment, because all addictions are rooted in the spiritual. They are deriving their power from the same source, emanating from that space within which exists beyond the five senses of our routine reality.

Obviously, the first step to turning around from an addiction is to want to be set free. Jesus would sometimes ask people whether they wanted to be made whole (John 5:6). If a person is stuck and wants to remain stuck, there's nothing anyone else can do to get them going in the right direction. Freedom from addictive behavior has to start from within. If you find yourself in a spiritually based trap in some category of life that has been inculcated with negative patterns of thought like a snake wrapping itself around your mind, you can choose a new direction toward freedom. But it has to start with you. You have to choose to get off the existing path and head in a different direction.

Your addiction is not an inevitable reality. You are not locked in a prison without a key. Do not decorate your cell and make yourself at home there. Do not fall prey to the lie that this will never change or that the best you can do is "manage" the level of your addiction. It is possible to be completely set free from whatever stronghold seeks to strangle you. But it starts with you eliminating hopeless thoughts of defeat, victimhood, and helplessness.

You are not the only person, nor are you the first person, to struggle for freedom. Even the great apostle Paul struggled with something he had difficulty shaking. In Romans 7:14–24 he laments those things he was doing that he did not want to do. His will was there to overcome it. He told himself not to do it. He was serious about overcoming it. But he still struggled between the pull of his flesh and the power of his spirit. The two simply couldn't get along.

Similarly, when Jesus raised Lazarus from the dead, we are told that Lazarus came up from his tomb tied up in his hands and feet. Just because he had been restored to life didn't mean that he was free. Lazarus was still bound. That's why Jesus instructed those around him to loose that which bound him so he could be free.

Life and freedom do not always come hand in hand. Many are alive who are not yet free. When the slaves had been set free by President Lincoln's Emancipation Proclamation, many did not know it for a number of years. Legally, they were free but emotionally, mentally, and even physically they were not. Paul speaks of a spirit of slavery when he describes our battle within in Romans 7:14–15. He says,

> For we know that the law is spiritual, but I am of flesh, sold as a slave under sin. For I do not understand what I am doing, because I do not practice what I want to do, but I do what I hate.

Paul summarizes what many people feel when trapped in addictive behavior. Addiction leaves feelings of doing the very thing you do not want to do. It can feel like slavery and bondage. Every slave has a master. In this case, the master is sin. Paul doesn't call it a bad habit. He doesn't refer to it as a mistake. He names it for what it is: sin. It's not just a struggle. It's not just a challenge. It's sin. And in order for you to overcome this stronghold of sin in your life, you will also need to call it what it is. The addiction you seek freedom from is sin. Sin holds the whip and rules you as your

Life and freedom do not always come hand in hand. Many are alive who are not yet free.

master. Calling it sin makes the issue spiritual and much more serious.

This puts it in a new perspective, doesn't it? This helps you realize that what you are facing will take more than a strong resolve or determination. Sin can only be overcome through a spiritual approach and a power larger than your own. See, when you are sick and you go to the doctor, the doctor is going to try to find the cause of your ailment. He or she needs to locate the cause so they can give you the right cure. What many people are doing in seeking to overcome addictions is trying to cure the wrong cause. They are medicating for something that is not the problem in and of itself. Typically, they seek to medicate the results of the problem or the symptoms of the sickness. But if you truly want to get healthier and heal from an addiction's hold on your life, you will need to address the spiritual root of the sin.

To understand this more fully, let's look at God's Word in 2 Corinthians 10:2–5 (NASB). It says:

> I ask that when I am present I need not be bold with the confidence with which I propose to be courageous against some, who regard us as if we walked according to the flesh. For though we walk in the flesh, we do not war according to the flesh, for the weapons of our warfare are not of the flesh, but divinely powerful for the destruction of fortresses. We are destroying speculations and every lofty thing raised up against the knowledge of God, and we are taking every thought captive to the obedience of Christ.

Paul tells us clearly what we are facing when seeking to overcome an addiction. He says that "we are destroying speculations and every lofty thing raised up against the knowledge of God." The Greek word for "lofty" can also be described as a "partition." I'm sure you've been in a room before where there exists a partition that can be closed in order to divide the room into smaller sections. Many of the rooms at the church where I pastor have partitions in them in order to reconfigure the room for specific purposes. These partitions are lofty in that they can go from the floor to the ceiling in order to completely create a new space for people to meet.

Now, the reason we divide the room is so that the information in one half of the room doesn't cross over to the meeting that is taking place in the other half of the room. We want the content to be separated so that one room does not interfere with the other room. Thus, what Paul is saying is that the reason many of us remain defeated is because we fail to destroy the partition in the mind. There is a blockage that Satan seeks to erect in the mind which separates the knowledge of God from the thoughts of man. When the lofty partition remains in place, the truth of God does not get through in order to inform and transform the thoughts of man. So, the Enemy separates your thinking from God's viewpoint on the matter. And any thinking that does not originate from God and His truth is thinking that contradicts God and His truth. It is, as Paul calls it, "speculations . . . raised up against the knowledge of God."

When God's truth no longer influences your thought patterns, you live in a state of perpetual defeat. The biblical term for this lofty partition and divided thought is "double-mindedness." It means to think in two different directions at the same time.

Consider what would happen if you tried to drive in two different directions at the same time. You would get nowhere, and fast. Similarly, double-mindedness keeps you stuck, trapped, and entombed in addictive behavior and thought-patterns that prohibit you from fully reaching the destiny and purpose God has designed for you to live out. One of Satan's main goals is to keep you thinking in two different ways at the same time. As long as he can keep your mind unfocused on God's truth, he can keep you bound and locked up in your consequences.

Satan doesn't care that you go to church on Sunday as long as he can have your thoughts on Sunday afternoon or Sunday night. Because if he can keep God's thoughts from penetrating the whole of you, then he knows that God's thoughts won't last long at all.

It's like if you were to go to a popular restaurant called Sweet Georgia Brown's in order to get you some soul food. You decide to pile up your plate with all the fixins, but, when you get to the end of the line and it is time to choose your drink, you order a Diet Coke. You do this because you hope that in some way this Diet Coke is going to cancel out all the sugar and fried chicken and carbs you just put on your plate.

Friend, it doesn't work that way. Yet what a lot of people will do is attend Diet Church on Sunday hoping that what they get on

Sunday will somehow balance out all the worldly thought patterns and activities they take part in Monday–Saturday. But the truth of the matter is that a partition doesn't allow for infiltration. A partition cancels out the knowledge of God, making it incapable of leading you toward your victory.

In order for the penetration of God's truth to bring victory in the area of whatever stronghold you face due to the vice-grip of sin being amplified by Satan and his demons, the partition must come down. The wall must come down. The fortress around the lies of Satan must be destroyed, not remodeled. When you understand this, it becomes a transformative truth. Unless and until you come to the realization that you have a divided mind, you will not have victory. The division keeps you defeated and unable to experience a U-turn in your life and circumstances.

So how do you bring down the wall? Jesus tells us. We read this in John 8:31–32:

> Then Jesus said to the Jews who had believed him, "If you continue in my word, you really are my disciples. You will know the truth, and the truth will set you free."

You are set free by truth. Now, this is not new. I'm sure you've heard this before. So let me phrase it another way in an effort to help it sink in. You will only be set free by the *truth*, not what you believe to be true. Truth will set you free. Not your version of "truth." So many are running around today talking about "my truth," or "your truth." Nothing is truth but God's truth.

Truth refers to the absolute standard by which reality is measured. Truth always sits outside of you. Truth is never defined, nor created, by you. One and one is two. One and one has always been two. One and one will always be two. This is a mathematical truth. You can feel like you want one and one to equal three if you want to. You can claim that one and one equals four if you want to. You can state that your truth is that one and one equals eleven. It doesn't matter what you say or what you think or what you label as truth. It doesn't matter what trends on social media. You can have one and one equals twelve posted by millions of people, but it will never equal twelve. That's just noise. One and one equals two.

> *Truth will set you free. Not your version of "truth."*

Truth is truth. And in order for you to overcome addictive strongholds in your life, you must conform to the truth as God declares it to be.

One of the reasons people stay stuck so long is because they are basing their thought patterns on lies. An enormous lie that contributes to this is that you can fix the flesh with the flesh. But Paul tells us in 2 Corinthians 10:3–4, the passage we looked at earlier, that we do not war according to the flesh. The flesh can't fix the flesh. Yes, you might try to manage it and get away with that for a while. But you can never fix a sin problem with your sinful flesh as the cure. What you must do is go first and foremost to the truth of

God's Word. It is His truth that sets you free. It is His truth that breaks through and brings life. It is truth that unravels the lies that bind your mind in a stranglehold of suffering that keeps you stuck in your sin and its accompanying consequences.

Seeking to release yourself from the stronghold of sin through your own efforts of the flesh can be compared to your grandmother seeking to clean clothes with a washboard. It would take days to do it, and still the clothes would be less well-off for the washing. They would wear thin and all the while your grandmother would be worn out, achy, and frustrated. God has provided the solution to our sin through the washing of the salvation provided through His Son. Jesus' sacrifice gives us access to the overcoming power of the Spirit within. The Spirit enables us to discern and receive truth. The Spirit helps us to do what Jesus told us to do in John 8:31 which is to "continue in my word." The term *continue* means to hang out, abide, stay. You must abide in the truth, not simply visit it.

Far too many of us simply visit the truth. We visit the words of Christ. We visit the presence of His Spirit. We come to church or go to a small group or read a verse a day to keep the devil away. But nowhere in Scripture does it ever say that visiting the truth will set you free. Over and over we are told to memorize, meditate, absorb, think about, consider, abide, know, and continue in the Word. If you truly

Jesus' sacrifice gives us access to the overcoming power of the Spirit within.

want to have victory over the sin and consequences in your life, you must remain in the truth so that its nutrients can penetrate your soul. You must do as Paul outlined for us in Romans 6 and 8: consider yourself dead to the lies and alive to the Spirit of truth. He says:

> So, you too consider yourselves dead to sin and alive to God in Christ Jesus. (Rom. 6:11)

> . . . if you live according to the flesh, you are going to die. But if by the Spirit you put to death the deeds of the body, you will live. (Rom. 8:13)

When you allow the Spirit to dominate your thoughts with the truths of God's Word, you will live free. As Jesus said, "You will know the truth, and the truth will set you free" (John 8:32). The word *know* refers to much more than a cognitive awareness of something. It means to be deeply convinced beyond any doubt. Perhaps you've experienced times in your life where you just know something. You "know that you know" it is true. It is a truth that resonates within the depths of who you are. That is what it means to know the truth and be set free.

Numerous times in Scripture this phrase "you will know" shows up, either rooted in the Old Testament Hebrew word *yada* or the New Testament Greek word *ginosko* as in the case of John 8:32. Looking at some of these other passages can help us understand what it means when Jesus says "you will know the truth." We read (emphasis mine):

> So Moses and Aaron said to all the Israelites, "This evening *you will know* that it was the LORD who brought you out of the land of Egypt." (Exod. 16:6)

> "Is it not the wheat harvest today? I will call to the LORD, that He may send thunder and rain. Then *you will know* and see that your wickedness is great which you have done in the sight of the LORD by asking for yourselves a king." (1 Sam. 12:17 NASB)

> "Kings will be your guardians and their queens your nursing mothers. They will bow down to you with their faces to the ground and lick the dust at your feet. Then *you will know* that I am the LORD; those who put their hope in me will not be put to shame." (Isa. 49:23)

> "Then *you will know* that I am the LORD, when their slain are among their idols around their altars, on every high hill, on all the tops of the mountains, under every green tree and under every leafy oak—the places where they offered soothing aroma to all their idols." (Ezek. 6:13 NASB)

> And I will betroth you to Me in faithfulness. Then *you will know* the LORD. (Hosea 2:20 NASB)

Then *you will know* that I am the LORD your God, who dwells in Zion, my holy mountain. Jerusalem will be holy, and foreigners will never overrun it again. (Joel 3:17)

"Then *you will know* that I sent you this decree, so that my covenant with Levi may continue," says the LORD of Armies. (Mal. 2:4)

"*You will know* them by their fruits. Grapes are not gathered from thorn bushes nor figs from thistles, are they?" (Matt. 7:16 NASB)

The type of "knowing" that Jesus speaks of which will set you free is that knowing that truly *knows*. It's not guessing. It's not hoping. It's not even testing. It is those times when you know that you know because you have experienced (in many of the examples in Scripture above) irrefutable proof.

The thing is, though, with God's Word we do not always get to experience the irrefutable proof ahead of the faith that is required to enact truth's work. This is why faith in God's Word carries so much weight and is so critical to the process of you overcoming any addictive behavior. You must first believe God's Word to be truth, then apply His Word to your situation as truth, in order for it to resonate and do its freeing work in your life. The truth helps you overcome your sin strongholds, but only when you treat it as truth. You must align your mind, actions, heart, and will under His Word and His rule regarding whatever situation or thought-pattern you are facing in order for it to set you free.

But you must know truth in order to align yourself under truth, which is why there is so much emphasis in Scripture on abiding in the Word and abiding in Christ Himself:

"Abide in Me, and I in you." (John 15:4 NASB)

Anyone who goes too far and does not abide in the teaching of Christ, does not have God. (2 John 1:9 NASB)

So then, just as you have received Christ Jesus as Lord, continue to walk in him. (Col. 2:6)

Now, little children, abide in Him, so that when He appears, we may have confidence and not shrink away from Him in shame at His coming. (1 John 2:28 NASB)

"If you abide in Me, and My words abide in you, ask whatever you wish, and it will be done for you." (John 15:7 NASB)

Many more passages exist which emphasize the importance of this same point. You must abide in Jesus and the truth of who He is and His Word in order to access the authority and power that gives freedom over sin. It requires aligning and abiding in and under Him by embracing, memorizing, and repeating what God says. This includes speaking God's truth to Satan (Matt. 4:1–11), and as well as to your stronghold (i.e., "mountain," Mark 11:22–24), and watching His Word slowly and surely detach you from your sin (Heb. 4:12). The freedom Christ gives is a complete release from bondage. As He says in John 8:36 (NASB), "So if the Son makes you free, you will be free indeed." Another word I like to use for *indeed* is *sho-nuf.* You are not somewhat free, you are sho-nuf free! Just like Jesus wasn't somewhat raised from the dead, no. Luke 24:34 (ESV) tells us He was, "risen indeed!"

That's the kind of freedom I want for you. And I know that's the kind of freedom you want for you, or anyone you love who is bound by addictive thoughts or behavior, as well. This freedom and new direction in life doesn't come through grit or grind. No, it comes through abiding and aligning in Jesus and the truth of His Word. That's the key to overcoming any addictive stronghold anyone struggles with at any time.

CHAPTER FIVE

Reversing the Consequences of Anxiety

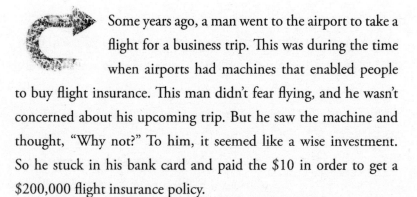 Some years ago, a man went to the airport to take a flight for a business trip. This was during the time when airports had machines that enabled people to buy flight insurance. This man didn't fear flying, and he wasn't concerned about his upcoming trip. But he saw the machine and thought, "Why not?" To him, it seemed like a wise investment. So he stuck in his bank card and paid the $10 in order to get a $200,000 flight insurance policy.

While waiting for his flight to board, the man went and ate at a Chinese restaurant in the airport. After his meal, he picked up his fortune cookie, broke it open, and read it. His face went pale from fright when he read, "Your recent investment will pay big dividends soon!" This man who had never once feared flying now felt a tremendous amount of anxiety about his trip.

It's amazing how quickly our emotions can change. A new report from our doctor, an envelope in the mail with the words "final notice" written on it, or a harsh word from our boss can flip our emotions faster than a surfboard in a hurricane. This is because our emotions are, by and large, responders. Emotions react. They move from influence to influence, leaving us with little stability at all. Worry, fear, anxiety, dread—call it what you will, it plagues most people today because most people have not yet learned one very important truth, a truth that will set you free: emotions have no intellect.

You do not have to be controlled by your emotions. If you've hopped on the emotional roller coaster of life, you can choose today to get off. You do not need to worry. You do not need to be anxious. You can stop. I don't care what is provoking you, irritating you, or aggravating you—God's Word gives you the power to walk away. You can disembark the wild worry ride rife with fear and simply go another direction. Your level of worry and anxiety is up to you.

You do not have to be controlled by your emotions.

Now, please don't assume that I am making light of life's struggles. I am not. I've been going through a challenging several years myself where life seems to be tossing curve balls out of a pitching machine straight at my heart. One thing after another presents itself as a point of concern. The Enemy looks to be throwing perfect strikes. But what I want to share with you in this chapter is that there is a big difference between concern and anxiety. Concern doesn't keep you up at night. Concern doesn't lead you down darker tunnels of "what if" scenarios. Concern creates the opportunity to seek a solution while anxiety seeks only to eat you alive.

I'm not saying you are to dismiss struggles or real issues in your life. Things need to be addressed. Decisions should be made. And concern takes you in the direction you should go. But what I am saying is that, as a believer in Jesus Christ, anxiety should never own you. Worry ought not to dictate your day. You are never to cave in to fear.

> *There is a big difference between concern and anxiety.*

A while ago, my daughter Priscilla faced a major surgery for some irregularities the doctors had spotted on her left lung. The surgery had been postponed during my late wife's courageous battle against cancer so that Priscilla could focus on her mom and our family during that time of need. But shortly after the passing of her mom, Priscilla knew she had to have the surgery. She shared these brave words with her followers on social media, emphasizing the spiritual principles we are about to explore together in this chapter.

Thank you for praying for me and for our entire family. We refuse to cave to fear, anxiety or a decrease in faith . . . because, well . . . ain't nobody got time for that! Through it all, we still believe God. We are trusting Him for a favorable outcome and that I will return to full health personally and full function in ministry.

Priscilla's heartfelt words expressed the truths we find in Matthew 6 where Jesus offers all of us the cure for anxiety. Three times He tells us not to be worried in this passage:

"For this reason I say to you, do not be worried." (v. 25 NASB)

"So don't worry . . ." (v. 31)

"Therefore don't worry . . ." (v. 34)

Jesus commands us three times not to worry. And when Jesus tells you not to do something, but you choose to do it anyway, that is called a sin. Yes, to worry is to sin. I realize that most people do not view worrying or anxiety as a sin. Rather, many people look at it as natural. They view it as legitimate, given the circumstances of life. Yet Jesus could not be more clear in that we are never to worry.

We are never to allow concern for a situation to develop into anxiety that rules us. Life brings us concerns, and we need to address them or come up with a plan to overcome them, or take them to God in prayer. But worry is when concern controls you. It's when concern doesn't allow you to sleep, or manage your temper. When concern devolves into a controlling factor in your thoughts and emotions, it has become worry. Worry is concern gone haywire. It has become a sin.

Now, before we go further, I want to give some clarification here about those individuals who suffer from a chemical imbalance, such that their physical and chemical reality produces anxiety. There are those situations where a person's emotions may sit outside of his or her immediate control because of physiological realities, and where medication to address the imbalance is needed. That is not the anxiety I am talking about in this chapter. What I am addressing here, and what God's Word is speaking to in this passage, are the times when life's circumstances control your emotions. Or when a fear of potential circumstances dictates how you feel about yourself, where you choose to be, how well you function, or even whether you function. It tells you if you can get up in the morning or if you should fall asleep early. It's when fear owns you.

Jesus gives us the antidote to fear that owns us. He does this by couching His command not to worry in a reason. At the start of the section on worry, He begins with these words, "For this reason I say to you, do not be worried . . ." (Matt. 6:25 NASB). In order to understand the reason we are not to worry, we need to back up a bit to what He said shortly before. We read it in the verses directly preceding it found in verses 22–24 where He says:

> "The eye is the lamp of the body. If your eye is healthy, your
> whole body will be full of light. But if your eye is bad, your

whole body will be full of darkness. So if the light within you is darkness, how deep is that darkness!

"No one can serve two masters, since either he will hate one and love the other, or he will be devoted to one and despise the other. You cannot serve both God and money."

One of the greatest triggers of worry in our lives has to do with resources. Jesus uses the topic of wealth to emphasize His point on how we get to the root of our worry. He says that if you want to get over worry, you've got to get rid of one of your masters. Worry will track you down if you have more than one master. If you have God as a master on one hand but something else ruling your life on the other hand, you will be torn in two. You will be pulled in two different directions, just as we saw in the last chapter. This lack of stability will invoke a constant consequence of worry and the instability that comes with it.

One of the reasons many of us stay anxious is that we are divided between masters. The spiritual division undergirds an atmosphere of stress and worry. Let me put it another way. The more heavenly minded you become, the less earthly worry you will have. One way to explain this is with an empty cup. If you were to pick up an empty cup, it would actually still be full. It would be full of air. Now, no matter what you did to the cup, the air would be there. You could turn the cup upside down and shake it, but the air would still fill the space in the cup. The only way you can remove the air from the cup would be to fill it with water. When you fill the cup with water, it will automatically remove the air in the glass.

This illustration can carry over to the spiritual life as well. The more of God you get filled with, the more that worry has to leave the environment. It is only when you remain divided between two masters that you choose to toggle back and forth between the antidote to worry and the worry itself. When God invades the space of your emotions, worry has to leave. Why? Because to know God is to know His nature, providence, priorities, power, and love. The presence of God leaves no room for fear. In fact, Scripture tells us, "perfect love drives out fear" (1 John 4:18).

Jesus sought to explain this and the path to take on our journey to freedom over anxiety when He used the example of nature. Following His command not to worry, He directed His listeners to look at the birds. He explained to them, and us, that birds do not sow or reap or gather their food for later. Rather, the birds rest in the reality that God feeds them (Matt. 6:26a). Birds don't have mutual funds, investments, or savings accounts—and they don't have stress either. Every morning they wake up singing. Every morning they wake up flying. Every morning they wake up knowing that food is there for them to eat.

> *The more heavenly minded you become, the less earthly worry you will have.*

How many of us wake up singing? Unfortunately, not too many. Most people get up complaining, sighing, and heading straight to the coffee pot. In fact, far too many of us face racing thoughts of concern which drift into worry before our feet even hit the floor. Perhaps it's a rehearsal of the previous day's issues, or a fear of what might happen that day. Whatever the case, few of us wake up as free as a bird. And yet we should be. Jesus reminded us of our value when He said, "Aren't you worth more than they?" (v. 26b).

The presence of God leaves no room for fear. In fact, Scripture tells us, "perfect love drives out fear" (1 John 4:18).

Jesus went on in His efforts to extract our worry by reminding us of what very little worry can actually accomplish. In fact, it can accomplish nothing at all. He said:,

"Can any of you add one moment to his life span by worrying? And why do you worry about clothes? Observe how the wildflowers of the field grow: They don't labor or spin thread. Yet I tell you that not even Solomon in all his splendor was adorned like one of these. If that's how God clothes the grass of the field, which is here today and thrown into the furnace tomorrow, won't he do much more for you—you of little faith?" (vv. 27–30)

With all of Solomon's billions of dollars (in today's money), he couldn't dress as nicely as the flowers of the field. Keep in mind, wildflowers don't get out a sewing machine to look as beautiful as they do either. Jesus uses an extreme comparison to remind us that we have no need to worry. If God ordains the flowers and clothes the grass, He will also care for us. He will also care for you.

The thought that rests at the core of our worry and anxiety, and the emotional and physical consequences that accompany it, is that we really do not know Who we are dealing with. We really do not understand the nature of God, nor the depth of His love. We have lost our awe of God. We think of Him as the "big man upstairs." And thus, because our view of God is so small, we find ourselves prone to worry and anxiety.

Did you know that God knows how many hairs are on your head? Jesus tells us in Luke 12:7, "Indeed, the hairs of your head are all counted. Don't be afraid; you are worth more than many sparrows." The older you get, the shorter your hair usually gets—but you still have hair. On average, there are more than 100,000 strands of hair on a person's head. This varies from person to person, but that is a rough average. Now, multiply that 100,000 of strands by over seven billion people on the planet. You've reached a number beyond one *octillion*. It's beyond numbers that you and I could ever even count in our lifetimes. Yet the Bible tells us that God knows every single strand on every single person's head.

He knows the ones that fell out or got caught in the brush. He knows the new ones that are growing in. If you are ever doubting God's love for you or His power over anything you are facing, just look at your hair. Or look at someone else's hair. God not only knows every single strand of hair of everyone on the earth, but He also knows every strand of hair of everyone who has ever lived and everyone who will ever live. Now, when you start to grasp that reality, whatever you are anxious about has got to look a lot smaller than before. The omniscient, omnipotent God who knows all can take care of whatever it is that worries you.

When someone is overcome with anxiety, they need to channel their focus off of their problem and put it on the almighty God who loves them. Isaiah 26:3 (NLV) says, "You will keep the man in perfect peace whose mind is kept on You, because he trusts in You." How do you live in a state of continual mental peace? You keep your mind set on God. You trust Him. You understand that He is bigger and more powerful than You can understand. And, being so, He deserves your faith. He deserves your trust. And when you put your faith and trust in him, there's no more room for worry.

Jesus told us that instead of anxiety and worry, we are to take heart, have courage, and be of good cheer. We read: "These things I have spoken to you, that in Me you may have peace. In the world you will have tribulation; but be of good cheer, I have overcome the world" (John 16:33 NKJV). Jesus said to "be of good cheer." Other translations phrase that as having courage, or taking heart. Whatever the case, it doesn't include anxiety, fear, dread, or worry.

Now, bear in mind, Jesus didn't say that everything is going to go super great and you will never have a problem. No, on the contrary, He said that in the world there will be tribulation. There will be trials, struggles, and challenges. But Jesus reminds us that in the midst of these things, we are to be of good cheer. Why? Because

He has overcome them. In the end, He has already won. And when you align yourself under the living Lord Jesus Christ, so have you.

The next time you are tempted to worry, I want you to look at it as an opportunity for God to let you see how big a God He really is. Paul described it this way in 2 Corinthians 1:

> We don't want you to be unaware, brothers and sisters, of our affliction that took place in Asia. We were completely overwhelmed—beyond our strength—so that we even despaired of life itself. Indeed, we felt that we had received the sentence of death, so that we would not trust in ourselves but in God who raises the dead. He has delivered us from such a terrible death, and he will deliver us. We have put our hope in him that he will deliver us again. (vv. 8–10)

Paul said that God allowed them to get to the point where they "despaired of life itself" so that they could witness that it is "God who raises the dead." He realized that God let things become increasingly difficult for them because He had a greater purpose at hand. He had a more important lesson for them to learn. In that lesson, they discovered that God had "delivered" them, and that He "will deliver" them. They came to know what true peace and joy is because they got a glimpse of how great a God they truly serve.

I was raised in Baltimore, and when I was growing up, we didn't have much money at all. My father was a Stevedore Longshoreman on the docks. His work was seasonal, so there would be months where we would live off of what he could earn doing odd jobs. Yet despite the lack of regular income, I cannot recall a single day where I ever worried if there would be food on the table. If my dad had to go out and catch the fish himself (which he often did!), there would be food on the table. My dad would have been insulted if I had gone up to him and asked him if we were going to eat that day. He would have been hugely insulted at the thought that I did not trust his provision. When we worry, we have forgotten who our Father is and what He is like.

Can you even imagine how insulted God must get when we question His capacity, ability, and intention to cover our needs? Now, I'm not talking about giving you your every desire. But when it comes to your needs, He will provide. Jeremiah 17:7–8 (NASB) says that He can provide even when it doesn't look like there is any way possible for Him to do so. We read:

> "Blessed is the man who trusts in the LORD and whose trust is the LORD. For he will be like a tree planted by the water, that extends its roots by a stream and will not fear when the heat comes; but its leaves will be green, and it will not be anxious in a year of drought nor cease to yield fruit."

Did you catch that phrase? It says, "it will not be anxious." No more anxiety. No more worry. No more drama. Even in a drought. Because God can cause fruit to yield whenever He wants to. He is not bound by the laws of physics as we are. He doesn't need water to make a tree's leaves green. Science has no say over God because

God is over all. So the next time you start to worry or be anxious about something, ask yourself if you've truly considered Who runs this world anyhow. The truth of God's care, love, and power ought to put your heart at ease. God knows how to arrange things, rearrange things, flip things, tweak things, trip things, and revive things. He knows how to do it in ways we cannot comprehend. Once you realize He's in control of even what appears to be out-of-control, you can rest.

A man was rushing to catch a plane one day. He had a heavy suitcase in one hand and a full briefcase in the other. Despite the load, he ran as fast as he could—weaving in and out of people—in order to try and get to his plane. While he was rushing to the gate, a man in a uniform stopped him. He asked him why he was going so fast. The man replied that he didn't want to miss his flight. So the man in the uniform asked him what flight he was taking. When he told him the flight, the man just smiled and laughed. Then he said, "You can slow down and walk. I'm the pilot for that flight and that flight isn't going anywhere without me."

Far too many of us rush around our lives like chickens with our heads cut off. We are rushing to fix this or rushing to work on that. We have one emergency after another stealing our energy and draining our joy and leaving us frustrated, aggravated, and irritated. All these are the consequences of worry for which we need a U-turn. But if we would just realize that God is over all and has it all under His control, we could rest. We could chill. We could take it easy. We could trust. We could be at peace.

Anxiety really isn't about what you may think it's about. At its core, anxiety has to do with the level of your faith in God. How much do you trust Him? The answer to that question usually shows up in the level of your anxiety and the depth of the worry lines on your forehead.

The cure for anxiety can be found in Matthew 6:33–34 where Jesus gives us the secret to living a life free from worry. He says:

"But seek first the kingdom of God and his righteousness, and all these things will be provided for you. Therefore don't worry about tomorrow, because tomorrow will worry about itself. Each day has enough trouble of its own."

We are to seek God's kingdom and righteousness first. And we are not to worry about tomorrow. Be present in today while seeking God now.

It seems far too simple, doesn't it? Maybe that's why far too few practice it. We often avoid the simple, don't we? Surely there must be more to it than that. Isn't that what Naaman thought when he was told to dip in the river Jordan seven times in order to become cured from leprosy (2 Kings 5)? Regardless, Naaman did what seemed too simple and, as we will discover in a later chapter, he got a great return on his investment of faith.

Matthew 22:37–40 sums up what you and I need to be about each day. If we will but focus our mental and emotional energy on carrying out the commands Jesus lays out for us in this passage, there will be no space for worry or anxiety to even exist. Jesus said:

"'Love the Lord your God with all your heart, with all your soul, and with all your mind.' This is the greatest and most important command. The second is like it: 'Love your neighbor as yourself.' All the Law and the Prophets depend on these two commands."

Put God first. Put others second. When you make loving God and loving others a priority, worry will no longer take precedence in your mind. There won't be room for both. The primacy, priority, and power of the rule of God over your thoughts, words, and actions will keep anxiety at bay.

Stay present. Stay focused. Stay at peace. God never promises to give you tomorrow's strength today. He promises to give you what you need in the moment that you need it. Far too many people find themselves crucified between two thieves: yesterday and tomorrow. They are troubled by problems of the past or troubled by worries of the future. But the Lord says to remain present with Him right now. Take one day at a time. After all, today is just the tomorrow you worried about yesterday. Let it go. Lamentations 3:22–24 urges us to do just that. God is our portion and He is enough. We read:

Because of the LORD's faithful love we do not perish, for his mercies never end. They are new every morning; great is your faithfulness! I say, "The LORD is my portion, therefore I will put my hope in him."

God is not going to give you what you need tomorrow today. When you get to tomorrow, He will give it to you then. You have to live in today.

Too many people forfeit today on the altars of yesterday and tomorrow. They sacrifice peace, rest, joy, and more all in the name of what may be. Whenever you are tempted to worry about something in the future, I want you to pray. Draw your attention back to where you are right now, pray, and turn tomorrow over to God. This isn't only my advice to you. It's Paul's. He writes:

> Be anxious for nothing, but in everything by prayer and supplication with thanksgiving let your requests be made known to God. And the peace of God, which surpasses all comprehension, will guard your hearts and your minds in Christ Jesus. (Phil. 4:6–7 NASB)

What did Paul say you and I could be anxious about? Some things? A few things? No, he said be anxious for *nothing*. Last I checked, nothing still means nothing. Thus, whenever worry or anxiety tempts you to let go of what matters most—your freedom to love God and love others in the present moment through a heart of peace—take that worry to God right then and there in prayer. Couch it in a spirit of thanksgiving because you know God is big enough to handle whatever it is you are taking to Him. Then let His peace guard your heart and your mind in Christ Jesus.

The psalmist said the same thing but in a different way. He wrote: "Cast your burden on the LORD, and he will sustain you; he will never allow the righteous to be shaken" (Ps. 55:22). Cast your care onto God Himself, and He will meet you in that space with His peace. He promises. You can take Him at His Word.

In fact, I would encourage you to do just that. Memorize these verses and then make a habit of obeying them. Then, watch worry diminish and disappear, along with many of its negative consequences. God is able to do all you could ever need, and more. But you've got to recognize that. You've got to realize that. You need to put God in His rightful place in your heart and on the throne of your emotions. When you do, you will see heaven visit history, eternity visit earth, and peace replace panic as God gives you your emotional U-turn. You'll witness God visit you in such a profound way that you can toss worry aside and replace it with praise and thanksgiving.

CHAPTER SIX

Reversing Emotional Consequences

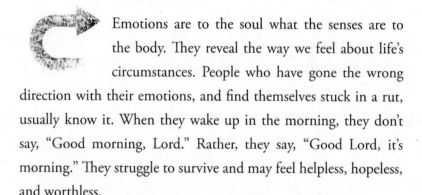 Emotions are to the soul what the senses are to the body. They reveal the way we feel about life's circumstances. People who have gone the wrong direction with their emotions, and find themselves stuck in a rut, usually know it. When they wake up in the morning, they don't say, "Good morning, Lord." Rather, they say, "Good Lord, it's morning." They struggle to survive and may feel helpless, hopeless, and worthless.

An emotional stronghold does not mean that you have a bad day every once in a while. It means that you cannot shake the negative entrapment that has grasped your life, resulting in uncontrolled discouragement, depression, and sorrow.

As we saw when we looked at the subject of anxiety and worry, while some emotional strongholds are tied to a physiological cause—a chemical imbalance or some form of physical need—the large majority of emotional strongholds are not physiological in nature. Rather, they stem from sin—either your own or someone else's. Maybe you struggle emotionally with guilt, shame, or regret over wrong choices you have made in the past. Or maybe you were emotionally, physically, or sexually abused, betrayed, or unloved. It wasn't your sin that created the stronghold you could be facing now—but it was still sin that brought it on.

At times, emotional strongholds even emerge from atmospheric sin. This is when sin so clouds the atmosphere around us that its results affect us whether we committed the sin or not (greed, social irresponsibility, injustice, racism, etc.). It is similar in concept to secondhand smoke and lung cancer. You may not have smoked the cigarettes yourself, but if you grew up in a home that was infiltrated by cigarette smoke, studies show that you have a higher potential for contracting lung cancer. The same holds true for sin. An increased environment of sin leads to an increased likelihood of emotional strongholds.

Yet instead of doing what so many people do (which is to try and deny or suppress emotional strongholds through pills, entertainment, sex, or spending), I want to help you discover the root behind what you are experiencing so that you can overcome it.

The truth is that God did not create you to carry emotional strongholds for five, twenty, or forty years, or for any time at all.

Rather, God has promised you, in Christ, a full life. Jesus said, "I have come so that they may have life and have it in abundance" (John 10:10b). He has not called you to live each day defeated. He wants you to know and trust that He is the One who is in control of all things, and that He is watching over the entirety of your life.

If you are not experiencing the abundant life that Christ freely gives, it is time for a U-turn. Turn to God and ask Him to reveal the areas where you are lacking trust and that an emotional stronghold may have set in. He wants to help you learn how to see past your sorrow—to view your life from His vantage point.

From where you stand, life may look dismal. Yet from where God is seated, all is well. One way to overcome emotional strongholds is letting go of the need to understand everything right now and trusting that God can make a miracle out of what looks like a mess.

Let me remind you again about something that is very critical: emotions don't have intellect. They don't think. They merely respond. Emotions have to borrow thoughts in order to stimulate feelings. Therefore, whoever or whatever controls your thoughts controls how you feel. For example, if you were to come over to my house for dinner and you carried with you an emotional weight of worry and stress because your bills had piled up, you had been laid off from work, and you saw no way out of your financial chaos, your emotions would be responding to how you thought about your situation.

Yet, if I were to hand you a check for $500,000 and tell you it wasn't even a loan, but rather a gift that God had told me to give you, well, let's just say your emotions would completely change. This is because your emotions are established and ruled by your thoughts.

In order to master your emotions and overcome emotional strongholds in your life, you need to master your thinking. When you align your thoughts with God's truth, you will be set free.

Whatever controls your thoughts controls how you feel.

For starters, living underneath the burden of emotional strongholds reflects a poor understanding of your identity in Christ. In addition, living a life bound by emotional strongholds is living a life of sin. Worry, fear, doubt, hate, anger . . . all of these, and more, are sins because they fail to align with the truth of God. They fail to position you at a place where you are free to obey the two greatest commandments we have been given—loving God and loving others. The apostle Paul touches on this concept of our identity in Christ being tied to how we live our lives when he wrote:

What should we say then? Should we continue in sin so that grace may multiply? Absolutely not! How can we who died to sin still live in it? Or are you unaware that all of us who were baptized into Christ Jesus were baptized into his death? Therefore we were buried with him by baptism into death, in order that, just as Christ was raised from the dead by the glory of the Father, so we too may walk in newness of life. (Rom. 6:1–4)

Take a look in the mirror. That person you see was co-crucified, co-buried, and co-resurrected with Christ. In the eyes of God, when Jesus died two thousand years ago, so did you. When He was buried, you lay in the tomb with Him. When He rose, you did too. Even though you may only have received Christ a short time ago, God took what happened to Jesus so many years ago and made it part of your spiritual reality.

How does this identification work? The process reminds me of the jumper cables I keep in my car. One side hooks onto the battery that has power, the other to the dead cell. Once the connections are complete, the car with the dead battery can be started because the energy of the good battery flows through it. The dead battery, through no action of its own, becomes "alive" again.

Back in the first century, the Good Battery died, then came back to life with all the power necessary to jump-start those dead in sin. The cable of the Holy Spirit connects your dead soul with Jesus' victory on the cross. The result: your spirit "turns over" and you are raised to walk in newness of life. Because of this reality, you cannot tell me that you cannot overcome your emotional strongholds. I know you can do it because I know who you are in Christ.

Yes, Satan is a master at planting thoughts in your mind and making you think they are your own, as we looked at in our chapter on anxiety and worry. I get that. Perhaps you do hear him saying something like, "I can't overcome low self-esteem and the comparison trap. I can't be free from this emotional bondage. I can't resist these old habits of falling into depression." He may say those things to you, or you may even say them to yourself; but in order to overcome, you must stop believing the lies. All those statements may have been true when the *old* you was alive, but that person died on the cross along with Christ. You are a completely new creation (2 Cor. 5:17).

Consider the appliances in your home. The toaster toasts, the can opener opens cans, the refrigerator refrigerates, and the microwave "waves." Each has a different form and function. Yet all draw power from the same source.

We are all to do the same. All who belong to Christ are tapped into the same unlimited power source, even though we look and act differently. The power that enabled someone else to overcome their strongholds is the same power available to you.

Christ is in the business of setting people free—and He starts with your acknowledgment of the truth that your new life in Him will enable you to overcome any lies the enemy has thrown at you over the years. You have the power, by the Holy Spirit, to overcome whatever is holding you down.

Handley Page was a great pioneer in the world of aviation. He invented a number of airplanes and his company contributed to the development of aviation in numerous ways. Yet one day many decades ago while he was preparing to fly one of his finest planes across the barren deserts of the Middle East, a large rat crawled into the cargo hold behind the cockpit before takeoff, attracted by the smell of food.

While cruising several thousand feet in the air, Page heard the sickening sound of gnawing in his small plane. Realizing that he was not alone, his heart began to pound. Hydraulic lines and control cables run throughout the cargo area. One misplaced bite could disable the aircraft and send him crashing to his death. There was no such thing as autopilot back then, so, being alone, Page could not abandon the controls to deal with his uninvited guest.

Sure, he could land, but from his current altitude, there might not be time for him to descend safely before disaster struck. Besides, touching down on the uncertain desert sand was risky, and his chances of being able to take off again were even more slim.

That's when Page recalled a piece of information he once thought mere trivia: rats require more oxygen to survive than humans. And oxygen grows rare as your altitude increases. Page pulled back on the yoke and caused the aircraft to climb high into the sky. In a few short moments, the gnawing sound stopped. Safely on the ground a few hours later, Page discovered a dead rat lying just behind the cockpit.

Want to know something very important? Satan can't handle the truth of God. Satan's lies and his darkness will dissolve in the light of God's presence. Climb higher and soar in the heavenlies as you reorient your thinking with God's perspective (Eph. 2:6). Sure, the air might be a little thin if you're not used to going there, but go anyway, because the Spirit will keep you alert as you adjust.

Keep climbing into God's mind-set and His perspective until He brings victory where you didn't think victory was possible. Keep climbing by rehearsing the truth over and over until that rat we call Satan and the emotional strongholds he dangles around your neck fall to the floor and die for lack of air. When they do, you will breathe freely.

One of the major emotional strongholds individuals deal with today is known as codependency. There are other terms that expand this stronghold to just beyond one relationship—those terms would be people-pleasing and social-media addictions. But, for starters, let's look at codependency.

Have you ever asked yourself who or what you could not live without? Some may make a list of material things. Others may immediately say that there would be no way they could live without their spouses. Still another group would think of the friendships they have formed and how endearing they are.

All these things are certainly God-given blessings. However, I believe we have mixed up our values by placing a greater sense of worth on things and people instead of God. Essentially, we often love the gifts more than the Giver, and become codependent on the very things God has given us.

Codependency is a coping mechanism (one form of an emotional stronghold) that enables a person to deal—albeit wrongly—with a lack he or she may feel. Perhaps there is a lack of self-worth and self-esteem, or strong feelings of being rejected. Regardless, codependency usually involves using a person or people to fix what is broken. I call this having a people stronghold.

God is the only One who has the power and the ability to meet our needs. The trouble comes when we insist on turning to others before we turn to Him. Throughout His Word we read how God uses people in the lives of others. However, we never read where God is pleased when we allow people and things to take His place. In fact, the opposite is true; we have created an emotional idol. Even an addiction to social media can fall into the category of emotional idolatry.

If that is where you look to get your self-worth and value, more so than to God Himself, it has become an idol. Likewise, if you allow other people or social media to depress you by giving you an untrue definition of who you are, that is a form of emotional idolatry too. You are complete in Jesus Christ (Col. 2:10). You are loved, cherished, and pursued by Him. You are accepted by Him. You are enough, because He is enough.

There exists a fine line between enjoying some relationship or benefiting from social media connections and the devolution of emotional relationships or comparisons. People and relationships are a gift which we should enjoy. But we also want to be careful that we do not allow our emotions to turn into a stronghold of depression, loneliness, envy, doubt, or fear.

Here are some questions to help you discern where God is in relationship to your other relations:

- When you receive news that fills your heart with joy, do you pick up the phone to call a friend, tell your spouse, or post on social media or do you take time to thank the One who has sent the blessing first?
- When trials come and the storms of life crash down around you, do you cry out to your spouse, friend, or post on social media first, or do you cry out to God?
- When you feel the need for reassurance about your personal value or purpose, do you start scrolling or text a friend, or do you go to God's Word in prayer?

If you will begin to make a switch in how you order things and go to God *first*, you will experience your dependence on Him growing while your codependence on others decreases. You will also discover that He knows how to send waves of encouragement to you through those whom you love, even better than you could have imagined for yourself.

Use the following steps as more ways to help you break free from codependence:

- When you find your mind wandering to someone else more than it should, shift your thoughts to God and His Word. Intentionally seek out ways to have fun—things that you enjoy, and not things that you think others will enjoy or that are dependent upon others.
- Pay attention to how you talk about yourself. Do you put yourself down or make yourself available for others to do

that? Reverse this pattern by affirming the things God is doing in your life through the words you use.

- Let go of the need to control your situations and, particularly, other people around you.
- Create a list that you either add to or read each day of things that you are grateful for from God.
- Reduce your texting and talking with those whom you may be codependent on.
- Write yourself notes of affirmation and leave them in your mailbox, or send yourself an email. You can even send yourself flowers or tickets to a ball game and remind yourself of the value God says that you have.
- Spend time with God before getting on social media in the morning. Seek to reduce the amount of time you spend surfing on social media as well. It's okay to unfollow or unfriend someone if you feel that staying connected is lessening your view of yourself and your identity in Christ.

Why should you do this? Not because you are the best person in the world or perfect, and not because you want to become self-centered. But because you want to remind yourself that, in Christ, you have everything you need. You don't need to hold out for something from some other person to make you complete.

When a basketball player has a tough time in his game, we say he is in a "slump." This is not unusual; athletes go through slumps all of the time. But an athlete can't just stay in that slump; at some point, he or she has to bounce back.

Being bound by an emotional stronghold, or strongholds, can be akin to living in a slump. You aren't able to accomplish the things like you know you can, or enjoy experiences like you were made to enjoy them, or even fulfill the purpose God has destined you to fulfill. You are still on the team—in God's kingdom family—but you are not living up to your potential. While it is normal and natural to fall into a slump from time to time, it is not normal or natural to remain there. You cannot stay there. You must be about the business of getting out. You must seek to turn things around.

Many of God's best servants went through slumps, and when we look at the stories their lives tell, we can discover some principles that got them out, and can get us out as well.

Moses, the man who wrote the first five books of the Bible, brought us the Ten Commandments, and parted the Red Sea while also delivering Israel from hundreds of years of bondage, found himself in a slump. Moses definitely contributed to landing himself in his first slump of many, but the powerful way that he overcame it is what I want to look at together.

Moses' initial problem was tied to people. He was hit hard by the negative emotions brought on through rejection. Perhaps you can identify. Maybe you have experienced rejection as well and are suffering from its resultant effect, low self-esteem. If so, take heart, because Moses was where you are, and he was able to overcome.

Moses' problems began right around the age of forty when he saw an Egyptian beating a Hebrew and decided to intervene

(Acts 7:24–25). When he killed the Egyptian and hid the body, he thought his Hebrew people would understand that he was there to deliver them, but they did not. Instead, they feared and subsequently rejected him (Exod. 2:13–14).

Yet not only was Moses rejected by his own people even when he sought to help them, he was also rejected by the Egyptian people and his own family. As a result, Moses was filled with feelings of fear and rejection, so he fled from Egypt and ended up in a foreign land. Forty more years passed by in this foreign land, and during this time, we witness a distinct change in Moses' confidence. The once self-assured man who was going to free the Israelite people all by himself no longer had any confidence at all.

If we were to tie what Moses was experiencing to an emotional stronghold, we would call it low self-worth. We see this exhibited when Moses encountered God at the burning bush. We read God giving Moses his marching orders: ". . . therefore, go. I am sending you to Pharaoh so that you may lead my people, the Israelites, out of Egypt" (Exod. 3:10). Great, it's finally time for Moses to fulfill his calling—he should be ecstatic. Wrong. Moses' reply reveals anything but joy. He says, "Who am I that I should go to Pharaoh and that I should bring the Israelites out of Egypt?" (v. 11).

In other words, Moses did not feel worthy of his purpose and his destiny. Not only did he lack personal value, but he also lacked confidence in his skills. Later on in his dialogue with God, Moses went so far as to say, "What if they won't believe me and will not obey me . . . ?" (4:1).

It was then that God told Moses to throw down the staff he held in his hand. When Moses did, it became a snake. God then told Moses to pick it back up by its tail. When he did, it became his staff again. God showed Moses that it was not in his own strength that he would carry out his destiny, but in God's. It was not up to Moses to be "all that"; it was up to God (vv. 3–16).

Likewise, the weight of fulfilling your destiny and being all that you were created to be is not on your shoulders. It is on God's. When you trust that and let go of what has you bound, you will experience His power. Your esteem should not be rooted in who you are and your abilities, but rather in the power God can manifest within and through you. In Him, you can do all things (Phil. 4:13). And that truth should give you great confidence.

Moses' rejection led him down a dangerous spiral of self-doubt and personal abandonment. Essentially, he allowed other people's rejection of him to lead him down the road to eventually rejecting himself. Have you ever done that? If someone else treated you poorly, abandoned you, put you down, or dismissed you, have you ever then wound up doing the same to yourself? Abandoning yourself and failing to give yourself the care, love, and attention you need is just as bad as other people abandoning or dismissing you. Don't compound their sins with your own.

You are not alone. You are valuable, treasured, and worthy of attention. You can overcome whatever emotional stronghold you face because you are not on your own. Just like we saw with Moses and his emotional stronghold of low self-worth stemming from rejection, God responded to Moses' belief in his lack of personal power by revealing His own power. God longs to reveal His power to you as well, but that will only come when you do as He says: let go of what you know (similar to the shepherd staff that Moses was grasping for so long), throw it down, and pick back up what God has anointed. Put your focus on what He can do, not on what you have done or what has happened to you in the past.

If you are suffering from the pains of rejection, I want you to remember these three things:

1. Your greatest need is not self-confidence, it is confidence in God.
2. God uses bad experiences for future ministry and blessing.
3. Obeying what God says leads you to a new, accurate image of yourself.

If you can empathize with Moses, then you need to also realize that you can get back up and start over—in God's strength, not your own. And friend, what is in your hand? Whatever it is, throw it down. Let God touch it. Then pick it back up again. With God, you can overcome.

The way to reverse the negative consequences and ongoing grip of emotional strongholds comes through awareness and a change of mind. It does not come from ignoring it or denying that it exists. You can't cure cancer by pretending you don't have it; neither can you overcome emotional strongholds simply by wishing them away. Likewise, seeking to distract yourself from them may work temporarily, but it will not bring about a cure. In fact, distractions that a person turns to in dealing with an emotional stronghold often eventually develop into their own strongholds (for example: eating, spending, drinking, sex, entertainment). When that happens, you wind up with more to overcome than just your original stronghold.

In addition, you can't reverse the direction of a stronghold by giving into it. If you feel like cutting, cussing, drinking, spending, or simply withdrawing from those around you, going ahead and doing those things will not help you overcome them. It will merely pacify you for a moment until the next time the emotion urges you to do it again.

Your key to victory in this area of your life is in acknowledging and addressing the root: what you think and believe to be true that is not true. When Satan is influencing your thought life, then you will feel what he wants you to feel. When God is dominating your thought life, then you will feel what God has designed you to feel. You get to choose who you listen to and whether you align your thoughts and emotions under lies or under the Truth.

How you respond to things in your life is most often a reflection of what you believe to be true. For example, if you doubt in your heart that God sees when you are wronged, cares when you are hurt, and has your best interest in mind, then you will seek to rectify your situations yourself rather than trusting Him and His ways to handle them.

Let me assure you that God saw what happened to you, what is happening to you, or what you are afraid may happen to you. Often what inhibits His response and deliverance in our lives is that we try and take care of things our own way with our own hands. This only compounds the initial problem, adding our sin to that which is affecting us. God is the One who will handle it for you if you will let Him. He is in control. He hears. He knows. He sees. He cares. He's got it. He's got you. It's time to trust, and move on.

CHAPTER SEVEN

Reversing Demonic Consequences

 When you are sick, you likely run to the drugstore to pick up some over-the-counter medicine for relief. We've all done that from time to time, only to discover that whatever we used didn't work well enough. After days of trying to treat yourself, you may give in—like I often do—and go see the doctor.

The doctor then does a battery of tests because he or she is looking deeper than just your symptoms. The doctor wants to get to the root of the problem so that the problem can be addressed and, ultimately, fixed. The prescription that you are given is often quite a bit different and definitely a lot stronger than the over-the-counter efforts you had originally looked to.

I would like to suggest as we travel down these paths of negative outcomes in our lives and seek U-turns to head in a better direction, that for many people, the reason why they are not experiencing victory and deliverance is because they are facing an undiagnosed reality. They are treating symptoms instead of the root. This undiagnosed reality operating in their lives might surprise you when I tell you what it is. The reason it might surprise you is because we have labeled this source in such a drastic way that we do not always recognize it when it is right before our eyes.

The reality is demonic oppression. Now, I realize that this is not a popular topic for the educated Western culture. In fact, it is my contention that we have educated ourselves out of a spiritual analysis of the issues we face. We have become so sophisticated that the subject of demons seems beneath us. Sure, we admit that demons may operate in third-world countries or in places where people are uneducated and live without scientific advancement. But in the land of educational astuteness like America, we believe we should be able to resolve our problems with technology and "modern techniques." Yet it is our failure to comprehend what demons are and how demons work that allows them to remain free to operate in our lives and circumstances at such a devastating level. Demons keep us hostage in slavery while we continue to look for over-the-counter solutions to a satanic problem.

Over-the-counter material methods will never extract Satan's influence from your situations in life. It requires a spiritual war waged with spiritual means to overcome a spiritual opponent.

"Know your enemy" is the first strategy for victory in or over anything.

Throughout Jesus' life and ministry, He had to deal with demons. When you read the four Gospels (Matthew, Mark, Luke, and John), He is constantly confronting physical realities with spiritual causation. Demonic oppression, influence, or possession causes more havoc and mayhem on this earth than we are aware of. Jesus confronted on a regular basis those situations where demons had infiltrated a situation only to bring destruction to a life or to a community because they were undetected and unaddressed.

One of the more well-known encounters of Jesus with demons can be found in Mark 5. In this account, we learn how to be more aware and acquainted with demons in order to address the undiagnosed cause of many (if not most) of the negative realities we find ourselves entangled with in life.

The opening of the story takes place when Jesus crossed the sea. We read about this in Mark 5:1–5:

They came to the other side of the sea, to the region of the Gerasenes. As soon as he got out of the boat, a man with an unclean spirit came out of the tombs and met him. He lived in the tombs, and no one was able to restrain him anymore—not even with a chain—because he often had been bound with shackles and chains, but had torn the chains apart and smashed the shackles. No one was strong enough to subdue him. Night and day among the tombs and on the mountains, he was always crying out and cutting himself with stones.

In this description, we see an amplified version of many manifestations of oppression today: self-harm, rage, recklessness, rebellion, and narcissism. These things may not be so stark in our culture today as this man's behavior displayed at the time of this biblical account, but the underlying reality of their existence shows up frequently in nonconformist and me-istic victim-based behavior.

The root of this man's problems, and the root of much of what we deal with today, both internally and with others, is mentioned at the start of the passage. We read that he was a man with an "unclean spirit." Behind the crazy actions and destructive behavior lurked an unseen spirit. This man's problem was not low self-worth or sheer madness. No, demonic engagement drove him in the wrong direction. This unclean spirit presented itself through him in forms that we would today sometimes label as trauma-based behavior, addictions, mental illness, psychopathic behavior, or other forms of self-destruction. And while medication may have its place when a true chemical imbalance exists in a human body, I would contend that many of the issues we face are often mislabeled and misdiagnosed. The spiritual operates in the unseen, and since we cannot see it, we frequently fail to diagnose the real root of behavioral problems.

But before we go further, I want to stress once again that I am not saying all mental illness is tied to demon-possession. What I am saying is that some of what we label mental illness is. The further someone finds themselves living out of personal control where their mind drives their decisions away from the compass of the Spirit, the more we need to consider the unseen influences of unclean demonic beings.

I also don't want you as the reader to skip over this chapter if you are not dealing with the extremes of mental illness, because Satan likes to subtly influence us in ways that are undetectable so that we do not face and defeat him with the power of Christ and the awareness of the enemy's ways. You may not be living a life as out-of-control as this demon-possessed man was, but there are biblical and spiritual principles you can apply to overcome satanic influence at whatever level it is you face it. Satan's goal is to keep us from living out the greatest command and ultimate purpose of each of our lives: loving God and loving others. Anything that prevents you or persuades you from doing either gives a notch in the belt of the Enemy's body armor. Whether it is bitterness, jealousy, apathy, low self-worth, or the like, if it prohibits your full expression internally and externally of loving God, yourself, and others, Satan has oppressed you successfully.

> *Satan's goal is to keep us from living out the greatest command and ultimate purpose of each of our lives: loving God and loving others.*

So how do we beat an invisible enemy? We start by identifying the enemy for what it is. Scripture gave this demon a nickname: unclean spirit. While it will be called a demon later, we begin by seeing the nature and character through this nickname. The root of this man's problems, and the root of many of our own problems, lies in the unclean arena where spirits roam. Demonic spirits are, by nature, unclean. Thus, for them to take up residence in your life or mine, they look for areas of uncleanness in order to enter in. They are drawn toward that which is in opposition to God, perceiving that space to be an invitation.

You do not have to give roaches a formal invitation to invade your home. You don't have to put up a sign that says, "Roach Resort." No, roaches will assume that if you have left enough trash or food waste in places they can easily reach, that you have invited them in. Neither do you have to welcome mosquitos into your yard. Just leave stagnant water around long enough and the mosquitos will assume your yard is their home. Likewise, you do not have to give demons a formal invitation. You do not have to send a note to Satan to let him know it's okay to send demons to your home. Rather, the demons will assume by the dirt in our lives that they have been welcomed due to the nature of their uncleanness.

It only requires a small opening to allow a demon to enter and make itself at home. Just like a few bread crumbs can attract a family of mice, it doesn't take much to attract demons. They simply look for where uncleanness exists and enter there. They infuse themselves either through influence, oppression, domination, or at an extreme level, possession. Demons amplify what is already unclean, making it dirtier.

Thus, the problems many of us are facing are not only the dirt we originally allowed through our own pursuit but also the expansion of that dirt by the demons who made themselves at home. That's why you can quickly find yourself going from a bad habit to an addiction, without so much of a warning. Before you know it, you find yourself captured by your own negative thoughts and behavior, influenced by demonic spirits.

What's worse is that the last place most people will consider when looking at how to change destructive behavior is demonic influences. After all, we are just too educated for something like that. Our Christian culture has become too sophisticated. As a result, we quickly dismiss even the notion of demons. Demons only live in rocks and trees in some far-off country, right? Not according to Scripture. In 1 Timothy 4:1–2, we read that demons inhabit deceit and twist our doctrine. They live in lies. It says:

> Now the Spirit explicitly says that in later times some will depart from the faith, paying attention to deceitful spirits and the teachings of demons, through the hypocrisy of liars whose consciences are seared.

Demons make their home in the immaterial world of our thoughts and belief systems. In fact, Satan is the father of lies. He is a liar from the beginning of time. He distorts truth to divert humanity onto a path of destruction. The demons who follow Satan in his rebellion against God are unclean spirits that gravitate toward lies. That's why it is in their interest to keep you from the truth because they feed on lies and what lies produce. They feed on bitterness, hate, jealousy, pride, ego, and vile behaviors. These provide them their sustenance and strength.

James 3:13–16 differentiates the outcomes of godly wisdom with demonic deceptions. We read:

> Who among you is wise and understanding? By his good conduct he should show that his works are done in the gentleness that comes from wisdom. But if you have bitter envy and selfish ambition in your heart, don't boast and deny the truth. Such wisdom does not come down from above but is earthly, unspiritual, demonic. For where there is envy and selfish ambition, there is disorder and every evil practice.

As you see, this is quite a contrast from the demoniac Jesus faced on the shores of the sea. While he was living among tombs, cutting himself and screaming uncontrollably, James lets us know there are other behaviors that come straight from demons as well—behaviors that look much less crazy and much more common. Bitter jealousy, selfish ambition, arrogance, and more can come from demonic influence. Anytime you take man's view over God's view, you have just invited demons into the situation. You have just opened the door for them to infiltrate and infest your life. It may take time to progress to the point of the demoniac that was so publicly displayed, but just because we don't always label it as crazy doesn't make it any less demonic. In fact, our culture often even congratulates and promotes jealousy and selfish ambition. Much of social media rests on those two pillars of demonic influence. Since the rise of comparison-based digital media has occurred, levels of low self-esteem, loneliness, suicidal thoughts, success-based anxiety, and other destructive mind-sets have also risen.

Demons don't always come dressed in red while carrying a pitchfork. Demonic influence is an invisible and spiritual issue that only gets worse when we allow it to fester, rot, and spread. Things in our lives (thoughts, relationships, activities, addictions) that go unaddressed at their spiritual core only promote a greater demonic influence within us. Before you know it, you wind up carrying out their bidding without even realizing they are the root.

The way to rid demons and their influence in your life can only be found in the power of Christ and His truth. As Martin Luther King Jr. said, "Darkness cannot drive out darkness. Only light can do that." You cannot overcome demonic influences through self-help strategies or New Year's resolutions. Only the light of Christ can cause them to flee.

This is exactly what happened in the case of the demoniac. We read further in the passage when the demon-possessed man saw Jesus get out of the boat, he ran toward Him and bowed down. He bowed down

Our culture often even congratulates and promotes jealousy and selfish ambition. Much of social media rests on those two pillars of demonic influence.

in a posture of worship and submission. Demons know Who is in charge. We read:

> When he saw Jesus from a distance, he ran and knelt down before him. And he cried out with a loud voice, "What do you have to do with me, Jesus, Son of the Most High God? I beg you before God, don't torment me!" (Mark 5:6–7)

When demons take over but Jesus is brought into the equation, there is going to be an internal and external conflict between what you want (freedom) and what the demons want (oppression and control). You can see this conflict show up in the way this man speaks to Jesus. He goes from using a plural pronoun for himself "we" to using a singular pronoun for himself "me." He went from plural to singular because the man is battling within himself. The demons were speaking and he was speaking. Both were looking for release from the torment.

What is the torment? The spiritual is meeting the spiritual. The spiritual realm of demonic forces is meeting up with the spiritual realm of Truth in Christ. When the problem faces the solution, it creates torment. There now rages conflict inside this man that erupts to the surface. In verse 8 we read that Jesus had been saying to the demons to come out of the man. But the demons didn't want to come out. They had found a place to terrorize this man and create chaos in his community. They wanted to stay, so they were grasping on to their hold with all they had. Jesus wanted them out. The man wanted them out. They wanted to stay. Torment ensued.

You may not have faced this specific type of torment, but you have no doubt been in a position where you were caught between two desires. You had an inner pull leading you to Christ and another inner pull leading you toward something else. You had the desire to please the Lord in what you did, thought, or said but something else kept pulling you in the other direction. Internal torment comes in all shapes and sizes. Torment erupts when the clash of the kingdoms wages war within you (Rom. 7:14–25).

Jesus' response to the demons' plea not to torment them was a question. He asked them their name. We find ourselves in the duality of pronouns again in the response. It says, "And he said to Him, "My name is Legion . . . because we are many" (Mark 5:9b). A "legion" was a group of up to six thousand Roman soldiers. This man didn't have just one demon influencing him by this point; there were thousands. Oftentimes that is what happens. You might see one roach in your kitchen, but if left unaddressed, you will soon have many more.

The more demons that influence a person, the worse it gets. The more addicted they become. The more they cannot control themselves, their anger, speech, passions, power-lust, and other destructive behaviors. That is because the more demons are in control, the more out-of-control you become as a person.

This man's demonic oppression had gone unaddressed for so long that thousands of demons had made their home in his body. Whatever uncleanness was in this man's life had drawn a crowd of more of the same.

An interesting point to observe about these demons referring to themselves as "legion" is that legion is a Roman term referring to a military group who operated in unison. They functioned together with one goal in mind. That's why the Bible makes such a big deal about unity in the body of Christ. When the enemy is operating in unity, it takes our unity in Christ to address it spiritually. We are more powerful than we realize, and one reason we fail to realize and access our power is because we remain divided. Satan's primary strategy is to keep believers divided. The devil keeps us fighting about race, politics, preferences, position, platforms, homes, marriages, and a multiplicity of things because our weakness is made manifest in disunity. If Satan can keep us disunified, he can control the agenda of the home, church, community, and country.

Even whole nations have demons assigned to them with the sole purpose of keeping those within the nation divided. They are to keep the classes divided, culture divided, races divided, and politics divided. But if you are too sophisticated to believe in demons and acknowledge they are real, you will be focusing on the wrong over-the-counter solution to a desperately deep and dark demonic disease. Legions operate in unison, as should we in the body of Christ. That is, if we want to experience the victory that comes through the power of Jesus expressed through us in faith.

Satan's primary strategy is to keep believers divided.

As I mentioned earlier, demons have territories. The legion of demons Jesus addressed in the man we are reading about in Mark 5 had their territory as well. When Jesus told them to come out of him, they begged him to let them stay in their territory. What's more, they even asked Jesus where to send them—into a herd of pigs. You may have never considered the demoniac account as an example of spiritual negotiation. But that's exactly what took place. Jesus told the demons to come out and the demons negotiated their surrender. We read:

> And he begged him earnestly not to send them out of the region. A large herd of pigs was there, feeding on the hillside. The demons begged him, "Send us to the pigs, so that we may enter them." So he gave them permission, and the unclean spirits came out and entered the pigs. The herd of about two thousand rushed down the steep bank into the sea and drowned there. (Mark 5:10–13)

The demons had to ask Jesus for permission to enter another host. See, demons are spirits. They are invisible. They function through living beings. They need a visible, tangible entity in order to express themselves on this earth. Jesus explains it this way:

> "When an unclean spirit comes out of a person, it roams through waterless places looking for rest, and not finding rest, it then says, 'I'll go back to my house that I came from.' Returning, it finds the house swept and put in order. Then it goes and brings seven other spirits more evil than

itself, and they enter and settle down there. As a result, that person's last condition is worse than the first." (Luke 11:24–26)

Jesus gives us great insight into the nature of demons in this passage when He shares that they cannot find places to rest (i.e., inhabit) in the waterless places. There is no life where there is no water. So they have to go where life exists in order to locate a host through whom to carry out their devious schemes.

Demons come upon humans so that they can express their uncleanness in our uncleanness, making our uncleanness worse than it was when they first entered. That's why by the time Jesus confronts the demoniac, the demons have become legion. Jesus grants their request to be sent into the swine. At the sound of His voice, they leave the man and enter the pigs.

The pigs, then, run toward the edge of the cliff and fall off, dying by drowning. The goal of demons is always death. That's their end game. It may not always show up as physical death, although there are times when it does. But anytime the demons can drag you downhill through the degradation of your thoughts, they consider themselves successful. They seek to defeat your life, unravel your dreams, and destroy your destiny. Their ultimate goal is always death, as is evidenced in the unclean pigs. The difference between the pigs and the man was that the pigs didn't have souls, while the man did. Thus, there was some resistance in the man that did not exist in the pigs. That's why when the demons entered the pigs, the unclean pigs immediately committed suicide.

A few years ago, I had an infestation of bees in my bathroom. The master bathroom had become home to a swarm of them. Dozens of bees would show up every week in the bathroom. This continued despite me going in there to kill them, spray them, or flush them. Every few days, no matter how many I had killed, more bees would show up in the bathroom. I was doing the best I could with what I knew to do, but the bee problem was only getting worse with time. That's when I decided to call the exterminator.

The exterminator didn't spend much time in my bathroom, even though that's where the problem was. Rather, the exterminator went up into the attic. When he did, he found a beehive. He promptly destroyed the beehive and sent me a bill.

Problem solved? Think again. Within a week or so, bees started showing up again in my bathroom. Even though I had called, hired, and paid the exterminator, I still had bees in my bathroom. So this time I looked for a different exterminator. I told him that the first guy had found a beehive in the attic and destroyed it, but this guy told me that the problem wasn't in the attic. He explained that we had been asking the wrong question all along. The question was not, "Are there bees in the bathroom?" Neither was the question, "Is there a hive in the attic?" The real question which would reveal the root of the problem was rather, "How are the bees getting into the house?"

That was the question he sought to solve, because, given enough time, if you don't solve how they are getting in, they will just build another hive. So, this exterminator asked me to take a walk outside of the house with him. We walked around the house a couple of times. He didn't say much as we just kept walking. Finally, after a few trips around, he paused and said, "There it is."

"There what is?" I asked, bewildered.

"There is the source of your problem," he replied.

At first I couldn't see the culprit, so he pointed it out to me. On the side of the house was a pipe. At one point, the pipe entered the house. Right where the pipe entered the house, there was a space. It wasn't a big space. It didn't need to be a big space. Bees don't require a big space. But it was enough space for the bees to enter and make themselves at home. Because that space had gone unaddressed, the bees were free to enter at will.

The same thing is true with demonic influence and oppression. What you and I have to do is close the gap that lets them in. We've got to seal the space—even if it doesn't look like a big space. Demons don't need a lot of space to make themselves at home in your heart. A little jealousy will do. A little bitterness will do. A little selfish ambition will do. A quick glance at pornography will do. Whatever the situation, you don't typically dive headlong into sin; it's a progressive devolution of heart, mind, and soul.

Once they have entered in and once they have begun to influence you, it requires a spiritual attack in return. It requires the power of Jesus. But just like Jesus did for the man possessed by a legion of demons, He can also rid any demonic influence plaguing you.

We read about one of the greatest U-turns in the history of U-turns, and it shows up at the end of the account of the demoniac in Mark 5. It says, "They came to Jesus and saw the man who had been demon-possessed, sitting there, dressed and in his right mind; and they were afraid" (v. 15).

Do you see what happened? It looks like a reversal of consequences to me. He has clothes on. He's no longer sitting near the tombs. He's no longer cutting himself. He's in his right mind. This turnaround took place all because Jesus overruled the demonic influences that had taken hold of him.

You may not have a legion of demons housed in you. You may only have one or two exerting a nearly unnoticeable influence. Or maybe a hundred. But whatever the case, you can be set free. You can reverse your direction. You no longer have to cave into self-destructive thoughts or pride-induced piety. Look to Jesus. Kneel before Him. Surrender to His rule in your life. Align your thoughts within His rule of love. Cast down every thought that opposes Him and His love. Take it captive. Close the gaps. Turn from the unclean behaviors or thoughts that you allow. It only takes a small space to let demons in, just like it only took a small space to allow an entire beehive to colonize my attic and home. Jesus has the power to remove the oppressive forces at work in your life, but it begins by acknowledging and repenting of misalignment from His rule in the first place. It starts with surrender.

I want to make one final observation before we close out this chapter on how to U-turn from demonic oppression. After the man had been set free, he implored Jesus to let him go with Him. As would anyone! But Jesus told him to go home and share what had happened to him with others. He sent him out as a witness. We read in Mark 5:

> "Go home to your own people, and report to them how much the Lord has done for you and how he has had mercy on you." So he went out and began to proclaim in the Decapolis how much Jesus had done for him, and they were all amazed. (vv. 19–20)

Jesus sent the man to the Decapolis. *Decapolis* comes from two words: *polis* means city, and *deca* means ten. Jesus sent the man to a ten-city region. He sent him out far and wide to share the great news of what He had done for him.

I don't want you to miss that. Each of us has a role to play in taking the truth of Christ's power to others. First and foremost, you are to experience His power yourself. But when He sets you free, don't keep it to yourself. Don't keep it just for your family and close friends to know and hear about. Testimonies of Jesus' power change lives. Your testimony is like a ripple on a body of water, moving outward to create a change in the whole. Your U-turn is never just about you. What Jesus does for you ought to be shared with others in an effort to draw them to Him as well.

Each of us has a role to play in taking the truth of Christ's power to others.

You have a part to play in the U-turns of those God places in your sphere of influence. You have something to say. If Jesus has delivered you from anything at all, you'd better not keep that to yourself. You'd better tell somebody. Then tell somebody else. Then tell somebody else, and so on. Do not be ashamed of the power of Christ at work in you. If He can deliver you, He can deliver anyone. You have a part to play in letting others know that too.

CHAPTER EIGHT

Reversing Generational Consequences

 All of us bear the DNA of our mothers and fathers. Our parents have transferred their genetic construct to us. We regularly speak about how a child looks like certain family members. You'll hear comments such as, "He looks just like his father," or, "she's the spittin' image of her grandmother." Our DNA determines the color of our skin, the color of our eyes, and the shape of our features. We are living reflections of the lives of our parents, physically. And we pass on this DNA heritage to our children as well. That's the way biology works. You would not expect anything different than for a child to bear the marks of their parents.

While we know and accept this reality as truth, what we often forget is that the physical DNA is not the only thing that gets transferred. There is a spiritual construct that transfers to us as well. This is the unseen makeup of spiritual inheritances that passes from grandparents (and even back further) down through the family line. You could call it a spiritual DNA of sorts. This includes generational patterns of sinful behaviors, strongholds, trauma-based wounds, scars, fears, and doubts. Whether we recognize we are doing it or not, it is a very real transition of soul-based scars that transfer from us to those who come after us in our family.

We also pass down generational blessings and favor, wisdom, abilities for insight, creativity, talents, and the like. But because this is a book on U-turns in life, we aren't going to focus on those in this chapter. I'm pretty sure no one reading this chapter wants to U-turn from the blessings that have been bestowed on you through generational gifts!

The negative consequences passed down generationally are a different story altogether. These negative repercussions of the inculcating of sinful patterns that we've inherited across generations can leave us bound when we never even knew why to begin with. These historical negative patterns create new negative results in our lives and in our world. Soon enough, we have enough negative results in our own lives that we claim these generational consequences as our own. Yet it is often the failure to realize and recognize the root of these generational consequences that prevents us from addressing, extracting, and overcoming them.

These generational realities come in all shapes and sizes. We talk about some people being a "born liar." They weren't born a pathological liar, but they were passed down the predisposition to lie as a lifestyle through a generational consequence and generational modeling. We've seen people whose father, mother, or both were alcoholics, and they also become an alcoholic. We see the breakdown of the family passed down either through a history of divorce or absentee spousal or parental relationships. Generational dispositions that form a negative repetitive pattern can manifest themselves in a multiplicity of ways. Children are not born racist. They pick that up from a genetic history of racism passed down through generational as well as through cultural and familial behavior that reinforces and trains that way of thought. They inculcate the pattern into their lives, thus acting out the transfer, eventually owning the transfer and ultimately passing the transfer down to their own descendants as well.

Spousal abuse is another generational consequence that can be passed down. Swearing profusely are others. Anxiety. Depression. Illicit and immoral behavior is another. The list is as long as the negative behaviors that are available for humanity to do, think, or be. Part of the reason is due to the process of absorbing behavior modeling as you grow up, but the other part is due to the generational consequences attached to the spiritual DNA each person inherits. It's a generational transfer. Scar tissue on the soul simply reflects itself over and over and over.

We talk about cycles when we are speaking of generational consequences. We talk about a cycle of poverty, cycle of abuse, or cycle of victimhood. Any pattern of sinful thinking or behavior that is passed down and then owned by the next generation is a generational consequence. That's how the cycles continue; with the passing of the behavior there is also the baton of results.

A lot of people do what they do, think what they think, and act as they act because it's been transferred. It's a part of their lives even if they don't like it. That's why you will often hear the statement, "That's who I am," or—even worse—"That's just how I was raised." These statements often come accompanied by a shrug of the shoulders and a sigh. They are defeatist statements if ever there were any. Because who we are in Christ allows each of us to overcome generational consequences.

Any pattern of sinful thinking or behavior that is passed down and then owned by the next generation is a generational consequence.

It's only when a pattern of behavior and thought goes unaddressed that it produces built-in results that go on to damage our sense of well-being, peace, order, stability, and hope. Generational cycles of sin will lead to more generations of sin, when left to its own.

In order to do a full U-turn from generational influences, you must first understand that God is a generational God. He refers to Himself as the God of Abraham, Isaac, and Jacob. God thinks and relates to us generationally. Much of the Bible rests on the concept of generational lineage, transfer, and bloodlines. Psalm 145:4 says, "One generation will declare your works to the next and will proclaim your mighty acts." We read about generations all through the Bible because God created the human race to generate life. And with the generating of life comes transfers of generational well-being or devastation.

Ezekiel 18:1–2 emphasizes this belief in and reality of generational consequences. It says, "The word of the LORD came to me: 'What do you mean by using this proverb concerning the land of Israel: "The fathers eat sour grapes, and the children's teeth are set on edge"?'" That was the proverb of the day. What they were saying was that if it weren't for what the father did, the children would not be suffering what they do. It's the all-encompassing psychological pinning of blame.

But God's response to the proverb lets us know that each of us has the ability to break the spiritual DNA we've been given with regard to negative generational influences. In fact, the more you believe the proverb, the more it will show up in your life. Yet God says He can show you the way out. He asks you to believe Him. He desires to show you where to get off this road of regrets passed down through generations. He says:

> "As I live"—this is the declaration of the Lord GOD—"you will no longer use this proverb in Israel. Look, every life belongs to me. The life of the father is like the life of the son—both belong to me. The person who sins is the one

who will die. Suppose a man is righteous and does what is just and right: . . . He follows my statutes and keeps my ordinances, acting faithfully. Such a person is righteous; he will certainly live." This is the declaration of the Lord God. "But suppose the man has a violent son, who sheds blood and does any of these things, though the father has done none of them. . . . Since he has committed all these detestable acts, he will certainly die. His death will be his own fault." (Ezek. 18:3–5, 9–11a, 13b)

Essentially, God says stop the blame game. Each person is held accountable for his or her own way of life. Yes, God is a generational God and often relates to people and cultures generationally, but He has also given each of us our own opportunities to choose. He relates both generationally and individually. Part of reversing negative generational influences is in recognizing the difference between the two.

Now, I can hear the objections already. It doesn't seem fair to be forced into a negative generational situation to begin with, like so many are. After all, we do have a spiritual DNA passed down to us and we do have modeling behavior all around us during our most impressionable and forming years. Much of our spiritual DNA and modeling may be negative due to the extreme dysfunctions in families and societies by and large. But what God is saying is that each person also has free will. You have a choice to think, believe, do, and be different. And since you get a choice, you no longer have an excuse.

There is another way of saying this. We all know that the definition of insanity is repeating the same negative actions or patterns and expecting a different result. When you and I are presented with the negative results of previous generations' beliefs and behavior, we have a choice to change. If we go along with the same behaviors and patterns while expecting different results, we are not living in the full power of God's wisdom.

It's true that we've all inherited the sin nature through Adam (Rom. 5:12, 15). And we all know that sin produces death, creating a cloud cover over the human race. But within our own time of existence, we are free to make choices. We get to make our own decisions. If we choose to repeat the negative practices of those who have gone before us, then the consequences of our choices are our own to bear. Yes, our ancestral line may have introduced the cycle of sin to us in various ways. Our parents may have modeled it for us. But no one forced you, nor I, to comply and do it ourselves. Our behavior, reactions, emotions, words, and beliefs are our own. We get to choose. You get to choose.

This is a critical truth that we have far too often forgotten. Generational and familial consequences work through influences, not force. You are not forced to do as you have been treated, witnessed, or experienced. But, as in the case of peer pressure, people often do the same based on conforming to what they know, see, and experience. A great example of this shows up in Acts 5. This illustration involves a husband and wife, but it reveals the reality of choice pressured by the actions of others. In this passage, we read that a man named Ananias stole from God and lied to God, in that he did not give to God what he said he would. When Peter confronted him about hiding his money rather than giving it as he had said he would, he lied about it. As a result, Ananias died instantly, on the spot. We read:

> "Ananias," Peter asked, "why has Satan filled your heart to lie to the Holy Spirit and to keep back part of the proceeds of the land? Wasn't it yours while you possessed it? And after it was sold, wasn't it at your disposal? Why is it that you planned this thing in your heart? You have not lied to people but to God." When he heard these words, Ananias dropped dead, and a great fear came on all who heard. (Acts 5:3–5)

Peter then called in Ananias's wife, Sapphira. He went through the same line of questioning. She answered with the same line of lies. Thus, she also died.

Sapphira had the opportunity to make her own choice. Her husband's fate did not have to be her fate. She could have spoken honestly and spared her own life. Yet she did what she had been influenced to do.

Far too often, we allow the choices of others to influence our decision-making to such a degree that we wind up sinning ourselves. At times this even comes out of a heart of love for those who are influencing us, even if they are influencing us away from the will of God. I don't care how much you love your spouse, parent, or family members, though, if that love influences you out from under alignment with God. At no time should your love for them draw you to do things outside of the revealed will of God (Matt. 10:36–37; Luke 14:26). Even if you wind up blaming them for it, you will bear the consequence yourself. You are to love God more than your mate. You are to love God more than your parents. You are to love God more than your children. God is the ultimate authority over all. The moment you allow someone else to trump God, you are out of order.

God specifically told Adam:

> "Because you listened to your wife and ate from the tree about which I commanded you, 'Do not eat from it': The ground is cursed because of you. You will eat from it by means of painful labor all the days of your life." (Gen. 3:17)

Right is right. Wrong is wrong. It doesn't matter who persuades you to do, act, speak, or behave unjustly. You are responsible for any decision you make that violates God's rule of loving Him first and loving others next. (See 1 Cor. 13:4–7 for a biblical description of love.) The consequences of those decisions belong to you. Loveless behavior breeds lasting consequences.

The key to discerning how to overcome generational traits and negative spiritual DNA transferred to you is through understanding the power of what is passed down while simultaneously accepting personal responsibility for your choices. When God says in Deuteronomy 24:16, "Fathers are not to be put to death for their children, and children are not to be put to death for their fathers; each person will be put to death for his own sin," He reveals to us our own responsibility that comes with the gift of free will. While whatever you or I may be struggling to overcome might have originated from the family line, God still chooses to relate to each of us individually. That's why I'm not using the phrase "generational curse," but rather "negative generational influences." A curse is something negative that is directly passed down, but an influence is something you have been given the option to accept or reject.

Loveless behavior breeds lasting consequences.

As we've seen throughout this book and throughout Scripture, the spiritual nature of sin includes demonic influences. When the demonic realm sees that you have adopted destructive generational behavior yourself, it piggybacks on that in order to exacerbate the behavior in your life to a greater extent. One way demons seek to do that is to cause you to believe the lie that you are under a curse, rather than that you have adopted a behavior pattern that brings consequences with it. One reason it is so difficult to get rid of sinful habits that we have absorbed and adopted from our forefathers is because the demonic realm amplifies the curse-mentality and victim-mentality so largely that many people begin to believe they simply cannot change.

You are free. You can choose. You can break the cycle.

That temperament, arguing, sensitivity, debt, pornography, drinking, relational disharmony, purposelessness, or whatever it is you face—you can be set free from it. You may have inherited a propensity toward these behaviors from your spiritual DNA passed down to you, combined with what was modeled for you, but it's not a curse. Jesus broke the power of curses over your life, and mine, by bearing our curse in our place. The book of Galatians spells this out for us clearly:

> For all who rely on the works of the law are under a curse, because it is written, "Everyone who does not do everything written in the book of the law is cursed." Now it is clear that no one is justified before God by the law, because "the righteous will live by faith." But the law is not based on faith; instead, "the one who does these things will live by them." Christ redeemed us from the curse of the law by becoming a curse for us, because it is written, "Cursed is everyone who is hung on a tree." The purpose was that the blessing of Abraham would come to the Gentiles by Christ Jesus, so that we could receive the promised Spirit through faith. (Gal. 3:10–14)

With the law of God came a curse and consequences. The law never provided a solution. In fact, all the law can do is show us the problem. It was never designed to fix the problem. God's rules showed us what was wrong, but did not give the ability to make it right. They were intended to expose you, not deliver you.

Many people have the wrong concept of how to approach God's rules. The rules of God, or the commands of God, are to be approached like a mirror. The mirror shows you what is messed up about you. It shows you what you need to wipe from your face, or fix with your hair, or what needs to be improved a bit before you head out the door. Without a mirror, you would not be able to see what you look like or be able to fix what might be wrong.

Similarly, the law reveals the sinful state we are in. The law doesn't fix our sin; rather, it reveals it (Rom. 3:20). But a lot of people go to the rules to fix the problem. That's a total misuse of the law. It's why resolutions never work. Promises never work. Rededications never work. Sure, they may work for a time or a season, but eventually your excitement and willpower will wear off. Unless there is true transformation from within, nothing will change long-term.

In the passage we just read, Paul lets us know that the best the law can do is condemn us. It came with a curse. But it is Jesus who sets us free. On the cross, Jesus broke the back of Satan. It is Jesus who, "disarmed the rulers and authorities and disgraced them publicly; he triumphed over them in him" (Col. 2:15). Jesus broke the curse. The devil can't make you do anything at all. Satan cannot force your hand. Yes, you may have inherited negative traits or dispositions, but you have the right and the ability (through the power of the Spirit of Christ in you) to turn around and go the other way.

Satan doesn't want you to know that. Satan wants you to believe you are bound. He wants you to feel stuck so you will stay stuck without him having to even lift a finger at all. But you are not stuck. You have the right, ability, and freedom to choose your thoughts, words, actions, and beliefs.

Yet while Jesus broke the authority of Satan and the curse of the law over you, He did not yet remove Satan of his power. Satan and his demons still have power, and they seek to wield that power in such a way that deceives people into thinking that with that power, they have authority. But Satan's authority has been stripped. You are free, in Christ. You do not live under a generational curse, although you may be living out generational consequences due to negative generational influences.

The great news is, you can stop and reverse generational consequences whenever you want to. It's up to you. God's Word tells us that the death and resurrection of Jesus Christ broke the curse of the law in order that God might give us the Spirit. It is the Spirit's role in your life, once you've accepted Jesus Christ as your Savior, to bring about the living out of the law. That's through transformation. The more the Spirit is allowed to influence your thoughts and will, the more in line with the overarching rule of love you will be. This is because as the Spirit grows within you, you bear His likeness. You reflect His character. Paul put it this way in Galatians 5:22–26:

> But the fruit of the Spirit is love, joy, peace, patience, kindness, goodness, faithfulness, gentleness, and self-control.

The law is not against such things. Now those who belong to Christ Jesus have crucified the flesh with its passions and desires. If we live by the Spirit, let us also keep in step with the Spirit. Let us not become conceited, provoking one another, envying one another.

Paul describes for us what a life looks like when walking according to the influence of the Spirit. He describes fruit. Fruit is an interesting term to use because, last I checked, fruit doesn't force itself to be fruit. Fruit doesn't strain, maneuver, or establish resolutions to be fruit. What does fruit do to become fruit? It simply abides in the tree that produces it. Fruit becomes fruit by remaining attached to the source of its life. You and I will reflect the character of the Spirit when we abide in the Spirit. You will break free from the consequences of the flesh when you choose to remain closer to the Spirit as your Source than to the people who surround you or came before you and influenced you.

If we back up a few verses in the passage we just read in Galatians 5, Paul explains how to break free of negative generational influences. It is done through the process known as walking in the Spirit. He writes: "I say, then, walk by the Spirit and you will certainly not carry out the desire of the flesh. For the flesh desires what is against the Spirit, and the Spirit desires what

You and I will reflect the character of the Spirit when we abide in the Spirit.

is against the flesh; these are opposed to each another, so that you don't do what you want. But if you are led by the Spirit, you are not under the law" (Gal. 5:16–18).

Essentially, you are to replace the negative generational influences with the positive, eternal influence of the Holy Spirit. When you choose to do that, you will be inviting the fruit of the Spirit to be made manifest in your life. When you walk, you simply put one foot in front of the other. Walking never involves standing still. If you aren't moving, you aren't walking. Why do I bring that up? Because so many people ask God to help them break free from negative generational influences and consequences, but at the same time, refuse to do anything about it themselves.

To walk in the Spirit is to move. At the point that the negative behavior enters your head—the desire to cuss, open the immoral app, contact the person you shouldn't, spend more than you have, put down or dismiss a family member, or whatever it may be—you must move. You must make the decision to move in the opposite direction. Walking involves continuous movement. No hiker ever set out on a trail and only went a few steps. Hiking a trail means you are moving along the trail. Similarly, walking in the Spirit means movement you choose to make in the direction of the Spirit. It means intentionally taking steps to please God and repent of our sins, while depending on the power of the Holy Spirit. This activates the work of the Holy Spirit inside of you.

Those who walk in the Spirit invite the Spirit's power to override the temptation or negative generational or personal influence present in their lives. If the same temptation or negative pattern of behavior shows up again an hour later, then you walk in the Spirit once again. You keep doing that until you are far enough removed from the grooves that grip your soul and your psyche that you can truly walk freely in love.

Is it time to break the cycle? Do you want to leave a better legacy for those who come behind you in this life? Do you want to be set free from negative patterns of thought or behavior that have kept you stuck in the swamp of sin, and instead begin new cycles of holiness, righteousness, contentment, and peace? If you answered yes to any of those questions, then you have already made the first step. You have made the choice to desire something greater than the sinful realities Satan seeks to throw your way. You can break the cycle, leave a godly legacy, and be released from negative patterns of thought or behavior. You do this by choosing to walk in the Spirit under the law of love. When you do, you will have broken the chains of negative generational influence in your mind, heart, and will (Ezek. 33:14–15; Zech. 1:2–4).

CHAPTER NINE

Reversing Discrimination Consequences

The subject of discrimination is not nearly as black and white as you may think. Yes, we often attach it to the topic of race. And in America, the racial narrative often focuses on the African American population and the white population. But while discrimination does and has taken place in this part of our culture, it also takes place in many more areas.

Take gender, for example. Women often find themselves facing a number of discriminatory factors related to work, relationships, and perceived value—even in the church. People can also be discriminated against in our contemporary culture due to their belief systems. Other cultural minority groups are discriminated against in multiple ways as well.

College students who seek to maintain a belief in creationism will face the discrimination of professors set on indoctrinating an altogether different worldview. Theologically conservative views, and those who hold them, receive much more discrimination than ever before. Business owners must now walk a fine line between their own personal beliefs and values and what the culture deems they ought to believe and value through their business decisions. Even churches are coming under a great deal of discrimination in the areas of what culture says is politically correct or not.

Discrimination also rears its ugly head between the haves and have-nots, no matter what color you are. I know from personal experience that adequate healthcare and access to the latest, most advanced treatments is so important when you or a family member suffers from a chronic or life-threatening illness. Access to the best in healthcare can make a dire situation more bearable, and perhaps even elongate the lifespan of someone who has been diagnosed as terminal. And yet, most people who fall into the category of "have-nots" do not have access to exceptional healthcare. Our country may offer a lot when it comes to advancement, but not everyone in our country has the opportunity to benefit from those advancements.

Even in the area of education, discrimination distinguishes between who has the ability to truly progress. The district or region a child lives in will have a significant impact on how well positioned this child will be by the time he or she reaches adulthood.

Discrimination separates. It always seeks to cause division. It serves as a tool of Satan to keep a large portion of society downtrodden, depressed, and lacking. God has spoken on this throughout Scripture. It's not always specifically called "discrimination." Sometimes it's called "partiality." This means showing favoritism or making distinctions based on preference. We also know it as "elitism."

But whatever term is used, God's Word is clear that it is wrong. And God's Word must always trump history, background, culture, race, and gender in telling us how we are to treat each other.

> *Discrimination as a tool of Satan to keep a large portion of society downtrodden, depressed, and lacking.*

James explains how our hearts ought to be toward the rich and the poor in chapter 2 of the book named after him. It's a lengthy passage but please don't skim it, even if you've read it before. Go slowly over these truths and let them sink in. It says:

> My brothers and sisters, do not show favoritism as you hold on to the faith in our glorious Lord Jesus Christ. For if someone comes into your meeting wearing a gold ring and dressed in fine clothes, and a poor person dressed in filthy clothes also come in, if you look with favor on the one

wearing the fine clothes and say, "Sit here in a good place," and yet you say to the poor person, "Stand over there," or "Sit here on the floor by my footstool," haven't you made distinctions among yourselves and become judges with evil thoughts?

Listen, my dear brothers and sisters: Didn't God choose the poor in this world to be rich in faith and heirs of the kingdom that he has promised to those who love him? Yet you have dishonored the poor. Don't the rich oppress you and drag you into court? Don't they blaspheme the good name that was invoked over you?

Indeed, if you fulfill the royal law prescribed in the Scripture, "Love your neighbor as yourself," you are doing well. If, however, you show favoritism, you commit sin and are convicted by the law as transgressors. For whoever keeps the entire law, and yet stumbles at one point, is guilty of breaking it all. (vv. 1–10)

That entire section of Scripture is about one thing: discrimination. Illegitimate discrimination is the ungodly and unrighteous practice and promotion of distinctions between individuals and groups based on faulty criteria. James wrote specifically concerning a spirit of elitism. The issue facing him and the early church at that time was in viewing the rich as more important than the poor.

James corrects this mentality, and we see Jesus correct this same mentality in the account of the rich rulers and the widow. We read about this in Mark 12:

Sitting across from the temple treasury, [Jesus] watched how the crowd dropped money into the treasury. Many rich people were putting in large sums. Then a poor widow came and dropped in two tiny coins worth very little. Summoning his disciples, he said to them, "Truly I tell you, this poor widow has put more into the treasury than all the others. For they all gave out of their surplus, but she out of her poverty has put in everything she had—all she had to live on." (vv. 41–44)

Jesus didn't create a false distinction and discriminate against the small gift of the widow. He saw the heart, and at the heart He knew her gift was even more valuable than theirs, because it was all she had to live on.

Elitism involves lifting yourself up as you push someone else down. It is not just a spirit of pride. It is a spirit of pride that leads to a misuse and abuse of others. James refers to this as making "distinctions among yourselves and become judges with evil thoughts" (2:4). He goes right to the root in revealing that the unbiblical motivation for discrimination is nothing short of evil. It's not just wrong. It's not a mistake. Discrimination—on any grounds—is evil.

That's what James revealed in the passage we read earlier. The issue was who would sit where. When those in the early church wanted to reserve spots for the rich members up front where they would be seen and comfortable, while leaving the poor members elsewhere, James called it for what it was: discrimination from the pit of the hell itself. Any motive that makes illegitimate distinctions deriving from a wrong spirit is sin.

Now, before we go further on this subject, I want to remind you that not all discrimination is wrong. We are told to discriminate between truth and error. We're told to discriminate between righteousness and unrighteousness. Discrimination between purity and evil based on a divine standard is part of living in obedience to God. But discrimination that judges, uses, manipulates, dismisses, devalues, or abuses another human being made in the image of God is evil.

What we have done in the body of Christ is we've picked up the attitudes of the world and brought them into the kingdom of God. Discrimination is wrong if it's allowed or authorized by man yet in contradiction to God. James calls out the believers in his day, declaring that they are in fact embarrassing the glorious name of our Lord Jesus Christ with their personal favoritism and distinctions. God's law to love each other as ourselves (Gal. 5:14) means there cannot be discrimination toward others. Favoritism and oppression are so damaging that Scripture openly condemns partiality in a number of places. Some include:

> "For the LORD your God is the God of gods and the Lord
> of lords, the great, mighty, and the awe-inspiring God,
> showing no partiality and taking no bribe." (Deut. 10:17)

> Peter began to speak: "Now I truly understand that God
> doesn't show favoritism." (Acts 10:34)

"Do not act unjustly when deciding a case. Do not be partial to the poor or give preference to the rich; judge your neighbor fairly." (Lev. 19:15)

"So I in turn have made you despised and humiliated before all the people because you are not keeping my ways but are showing partiality in your instruction." (Mal. 2:9)

There is no Jew or Greek, slave or free, male and female; since you are all one in Christ Jesus. (Gal. 3:28)

For there is no favoritism with God. (Rom. 2:11)

How you treat people reveals how you view God. Illegitimate discrimination reflects a darkened spirit toward God because humanity is made in the image of God. When you press the wrong note on a piano, you bring discord to the whole song. When you have dirt on your shirt in just one spot, you have to wash the whole shirt. When you have a crack in your windshield, you say that your window is broken, because that one crack has messed up the whole thing, and you have to replace the entire windshield. Similarly, when you violate this one area of God's law of love, you have broken the whole law of God (James 2:10). You have disrupted the rule of God throughout humanity and sent shock waves of discord instead of unity.

Since this book is about how to overcome the consequences of negative behaviors (either done by you or to you), I'm not going to spend a lot of time on the various types of discrimination. Many of us have either been discriminated against or have discriminated against someone else. Unfortunately, most of us have probably experienced both. So whether you need to reverse the results of discrimination brought against you or whether you need to repent of your own partiality toward others and treat everyone equally in love, the road map to personal equity (given or received) is marked by love.

Areas of discrimination include race, gender, belief, politics, culture, preferences, and even age. The ungodly devaluing of anyone is wrong. God values every single person equally. When it comes to the kingdom of God, the Bible is clear that we are all made in the image of God. To downgrade, ignore, dismiss or under-use someone simply due to their color, gender, age, class, education, or personality is sin. Even judging people because they have different preferences than you is sin. The entire chapter of Romans 14 deals with preferential discrimination. When you judge someone because they don't like what you like or they do like what you don't, that's sin. And remember, sin always comes with consequences. People have the right to be different than you. You have a right to be different than others. The apostles were different from each other. If God wanted everyone to be the same, He would have made us the same.

In addition, people are on different paths when it comes to spiritual growth. We are not all at the same spiritual level of maturity. To judge someone for lacking wisdom where you may have already gained it is actually to lack wisdom, because that is to sin. I won't include the entire chapter of Romans 14 here but I encourage you to read it. You'll gather the sentiment behind the Scripture in these verses:

> Welcome anyone who is weak in faith, but don't argue about disputed matters. One person believes he may eat anything, while one who is weak eats only vegetables. One who eats must not look down on one who does not eat, and one who does not eat must not judge one who does, because God has accepted him. . . .
>
> But you, why do you judge your brother or sister? Or you, why do you despise your brother or sister? For we will all stand before the judgment seat of God. . . . Therefore, let us no longer judge one another. Instead decide never to put a stumbling block or pitfall in a the way of your brother or sister. . . .
>
> Do not tear down God's work because of food. Everything is clean, but it is wrong to make someone fall by what he eats. It is a good thing not to eat meat, or to drink wine, or do anything that makes your brother or sister stumble. Whatever you believe about these things, keep between yourself and God. Blessed is the one who does not condemn himself by what he approves. But whoever doubts stands condemned if he eats, because his eating is not from faith, and everything that is not from faith is sin. (Rom. 14:1–3, 10, 13, 20–23)

Paul reminds us in this passage that some people prefer certain things and their conscience allows for it. People are different, and we must allow for the freedom to be different, because where there exists illegitimate division, there also exists divine judgment. Illegitimate discrimination (judging others) invites divine wrath. Division promotes chaos. The chaos prevalent in our culture today reflects this spirit of division that Satan has been allowed to promote. Anytime we deviate from God's command for unity (oneness of purpose), we are serving another kingdom. We are promoting the kingdom of Satan himself.

Galatians 5:14 says that the entirety of the law can be summarized in this one concept: "Love your neighbor as yourself." In James 2, the passage we looked at as we started this chapter, James refers to this law of love as "the royal law" (v. 8). It is the supreme rule which is to govern our hearts, thoughts, words, and actions. Royal means kingly. The law of love and, thus, unity, is royal because it comes from the King. It is the superimposing of His own heart over ours.

Division promotes chaos.

Love is the chief rule that brings together all other rules. I define love as compassionately, righteously, and responsibly meeting the needs of another. It includes pursuing the well-being of another—whether that well-being is emotional, physical, psychological, educational, spiritual, tangible, or more.

The reverse of this law of love means pursuing your own well-being, above and beyond that of others. It can even include pursuing it at the expense of others. The entirety of disobedience and rebellion can be summarized by division. Division comes through hatred, discrimination, pride, elitism, and oppression. Division breeds disunity, conflict, fear, and anxiety. It also gives cause to divine negative consequences on individuals, families, churches, and communities.

Love breeds harmony, peace, equity, calm, and cooperation. It also gives cause to divine blessing. How you treat others plays a part in how you are treated by God. It is a principle that I often refer to as living like a horizontal Jesus. What you do horizontally with others will often impact what God does vertically in His relationship with you. It's a boomerang principle we read about in Luke 6:38 where it says, "Give, and it will be given to you; a good measure—pressed down, shaken together, and running over—will be poured into your lap. For with the measure you use, it will be measured back to you."

What many people don't realize in this passage is that what you give is very important. Because the thing you give will boomerang back to you. Thus, if you need it—give it. If you need financial healing or restoration, then give to someone else who needs it too. If you need relational connection, then look for ways you could give to someone who is lonely as well (maybe that is an elderly person in a care facility). The boomerang effect of what you do will return to you.

I talk about this in greater depth in my book *Experiencing God Together: How Your Connection with Others Deepens Your Relationship with God*. In it, I explain how a lot of people look to God to rectify or reverse negative situations in their own life but fail to realize how God wants to use them to minister to someone else as well. After all, we are to be the hands and feet of Jesus (2 Cor. 5:18–19).

A lot of us are calling on God to do things for us that He is never going to do because He sees what we do—and don't do—to others. He sees our elitism, classism, genderism, racism, or plain discrimination based on preferences or personalities. God has made it clear that He is not a God of partiality, so when we choose to live our lives with favoritism toward certain people and disdain for others, we have chosen to violate His rule of love. Our rebellion can only boomerang the consequences of that rebellion in return.

Living in alignment underneath the royal law of love releases life back to you. It releases joy back to you. It releases freedom, value, esteem, and opportunity back to you. Blessing others opens the floodgate for God to bless you. Deuteronomy 24 lays out the cause-and-effect relationship this way:

"When you make a loan of any kind to your neighbor, do not enter his house to collect what he offers as security. Stand outside while the man you are making the loan to brings the security out to you. If he is a poor man, do not sleep with the garment he has given as security. Be sure to return it to him at sunset. Then he will sleep in it and bless you, and this will be counted as righteousness to you before the LORD your God.

"Do not oppress a hired worker who is poor and needy, whether one of your Israelite brothers or one of the resident aliens in a town in your land. You are to pay him his wages each day before the sun sets, because he is poor and depends on them. Otherwise he will cry out to the LORD against you, and you will be held guilty. . . . When you reap the harvest in your field, and you forget a sheaf in the field, do not go back to get it. It is to be left for the resident alien, the fatherless, and the widow, so that the LORD your God may bless you in all the work of your hands." (vv. 10–15, 19)

Did you catch that phrase at the end of the passage? It says that these things were to be done "so that the LORD your God may bless you in all the work of your hands." When you help others, you are really helping yourself as well. The way God relates to you and me is tied to how we relate to others. Discrimination is not just a sin against someone else. When you choose to show favoritism toward someone or discriminate against someone, you are doing this to your own detriment. If you desire for God to bless you, you need to bless others. Particularly those others who cannot pay you back themselves.

Jesus put it this way:

"When you host a banquet, invite those who are poor, maimed, lame, or blind. And you will be blessed, because they cannot repay you; for you will be repaid at the resurrection of the righteous." (Luke 14:13–14)

And lest you toss this truth aside in favor of myopic, short-term benefits, thinking that heaven is just too far away to care right at this moment, please know that you will not just receive rewards in eternity, but now as well (Mark 10:29–31). You get both. But it's tied to how you treat others. Discrimination toward others, on any grounds, will lead you down the path of personal destruction. A pure love that values and esteems all will lead you to a life of reward.

Never forget that the Bible tells us many have entertained angels without even knowing it (Heb. 13:2). Your treatment of others is a litmus test of your heart for God. God's heart for the poor and the disadvantaged is great. He is a God of deliverance. He cares for the oppressed. In fact, we are told that He blesses the poor with great faith. As we saw earlier when we looked at James 2:5, "Didn't God choose the poor in this world to be rich in faith and heirs of the kingdom that he has promised to those who love him?"

I understand that you may have faced discrimination in your lifetime and that it hurts. Trust me, I know how discrimination feels. I know what it is like to have a professor where I studied tell me I cannot come to his church due to the color of my skin. I have had doors literally close in my face as those who claim to know and serve Christ tell me that I, and my wife, are not welcome to worship there. I've been passed over, underrated, judged, belittled, and more.

What's worse, I had to experience my kids going through some of that as well when they were growing up. Once when my daughter Priscilla was the only African American on the cheer squad, one of the moms held a party for her daughter and invited everyone but Priscilla. We know discrimination firsthand. I can feel your pain if your story resembles mine in any way, due to anything that is out of your immediate control, such as your class, gender, education, race, or more.

> *Your treatment of others is a litmus test of your heart for God.*

Yet despite the pain you or I felt, we will still be held accountable before God if we ever discriminate against someone else. You can't point the blame at what has been done to you as an excuse for what you do toward others. The consequences that have shown up in your life because of any preferential or oppressive treatment you've shown to others are yours alone to bear. Similarly, the blessing that has shown up in your life due to the love and equity you've shown to others is yours to experience and enjoy.

James concludes his earlier summation of discrimination by stating, "For judgment is without mercy to the one who has not shown mercy. Mercy triumphs over judgment" (James 2:13). Judgment will have no mercy to the one who discriminates. When you live your life so self-absorbed, God's Word says that judgment will be merciless when it comes time to render an account for your life (Matt. 12:36). If how you roll involves rolling right over others, then the moment you realize how desperately you need mercy, you will only find judgment. When you need someone to cover your back, there will be no one there. When you are in a position to throw yourself on the mercy of the court, it will be too late. This is because God looks at your mercy-record in determining how much to give to you. He looks at how well you loved others made in His image in order to establish the flow of your own mercy and blessing. This applies in the life that is now and in the life to come.

When you and I get to heaven, we will have to give an account for all that we did. God is going to play our tape, so to speak. He will evaluate our words, deeds, thoughts, and actions. What we did will determine the level of reward (or lack thereof) that we receive. Keep in mind, what you do has no bearing on whether you enter eternity in heaven. Your salvation is based solely on the blood of Jesus Christ through His sacrificial atonement. But what you did on this earth will play a large part on the reward—or the loss of reward—you get in heaven.

Now, you may want to skip that section. But the Bible is clear that we will all be held to account at the judgment seat of Christ. None of us get to skip it. We will each sit with the Lord and review our lives. What the verse means that we just looked at in James 2:13 is that if you withheld mercy and love from others, you will be judged without mercy. But if we showed love through equity, through non-discriminatory behavior and words, we will receive mercy.

As we read in 1 Peter, that mercy can even apply to our sins. Talk about a reversal! Talk about how to turn things around and make a U-turn in your life! God gives you the very directions to do just that. You need to get off on the love-loop in order to turn around and go the other direction from discrimination and division. Scripture says, "Above all, maintain constant love for one another, since love covers a multitude of sins" (1 Pet. 4:8).

Love covers sins. Mercy triumphs over judgment. God looks for the redeemable thoughts, words, and actions in your life in order to show you mercy where you need it most. He wants to show you mercy both in time and in eternity. But because He is a God of love, His mercy comes tied to your love for others. Build your mercy portfolio by loving others. Invest in your own spiritual state of being by investing in others. Defeat discrimination and division by unifying with others in a heart of love.

Pursue the well-being of those around you—especially those who have no one to speak on their behalf (Prov. 31:9; Ps. 82:3). When you make this your passion and pattern in life, you will have set yourself on the pathway to living out the full manifestation of your divine design. You will have positioned yourself to experience the goodness of God in the land of the living (Ps. 27:13). You will know what it means to have the abundant life Jesus came to give as well as experience His mercy as He reverses consequences in your own life.

CHAPTER TEN

Reversing Financial Consequences

 The addiction to debt in our contemporary culture has become a new form of slavery. Most people's song when they get up to go to work in the morning goes like this: "I owe, I owe, so off to work I go!" People have inherited a lifestyle of debt. It's promoted and pushed everywhere you turn—whether through stores, advertising, social media, or the like. The concept of spending before you get, or even spending more than you get, has become commonplace.

It has been stated that there are three types of people: the haves, the have-nots, and the have-not-paid-for-what-they-haves. The last group has grown exponentially in the last few decades. As a result, debt has become the new driver in our decisions.

It may sound harsh, but Scripture calls it debt slavery. MasterCard has become Massah Card and Visa now means: Voluntary Institutional Slavery Always. In Proverbs 22:7 we read: "The rich rule over the poor, and the borrower is a slave to the lender." To be a slave means you have lost your ability to choose. You are now dictated by some external force as to what you do. When debt looms large in a person's life, it can dictate important life choices like where you work, what you do, what you eat, and what you can enjoy.

The biblical account that will serve as the backdrop for what we learn in this chapter on how to reverse financial consequences is in 2 Kings 4. In this passage, we come to know a single mother who can no longer pay her bills. Her husband has died and, as a result, she cannot make ends meet. Finding herself subjected to creditors, she has fallen into a state of panic.

In biblical times, creditors did much more than annoy you with phone calls or send notices to collect. In biblical times the creditors had a right to take your children away to work as slave labor until your debt had been paid. We get a glimpse that this is exactly what this widow is facing when we read in 2 Kings 4:1:

> One of the wives of the sons of the prophets cried out to Elisha, "Your servant, my husband, has died. You know that your servant feared the LORD. Now the creditor is coming to take my two children as his slaves."

This woman faced an insurmountable challenge. Her husband had died, and now she was about to lose her two children to slavery as well. To say that she needed a U-turn in her life, quickly, would be an understatement. Financial insecurity had led to emotional and even physical insecurity.

When debt and financial distress present themselves in a home, the entire family can be affected on a number of levels. Many couples or parents know what it is to be disturbed by bills. As a pastor, I have the honor of counseling a good number of married couples. No surprise to you, I'm sure, but the number-one reason why couples go into marriage counseling has to do with financial stress. When debt roars, it often does so with such strength that it carves out a dividing cavern in the relationship.

Unfortunately, far too many people today live their lives paying for the past rather than planning for the future. Financial insecurity and debt have become a crisis not only for individuals and families, but similarly for our nation and the world.

Let me be completely clear as we start our time together on this sensitive subject: illegitimate debt should be abnormal. Illegitimate debt should never be the norm in a person's, family's, or nation's state of being. Therefore, if you are living in debt, with more month than money, on an ongoing basis, you are living outside of the will of God. God makes it clear in Psalm 37:21, "The wicked person borrows and does not repay . . ." The Bible labels it wickedness to have bills that you are unable to pay.

Now, having no debt does not mean an absence of bills. It doesn't mean you don't have a car loan or a mortgage. Also, there are times when things happen outside of our control (i.e., serious illness, natural disasters, etc.) that can create a legitimate debt. But illegitimate debt refers to having more bills than money to service the debt due to greed, lack of contentment, poor financial planning, or ignorance of God's plan for handling our finances. It means having bills that you cannot pay because of your foolish decisions. If you are regularly past due on debt, then something needs to be corrected.

Illegitimate debt should be abnormal.

Like the widow facing the creditors, you also need a U-turn. Your consequences may not appear as drastic or tangible as hers, but keep in mind that spiritual, emotional, relational, and even physical consequences reveal themselves often in subtle ways. What's more, they become cyclical. To not address the debt situation in your life would be entirely unwise. That's why I've chosen it as one of our subjects to look at in this book on making U-turns in your life.

The primary lesson we can learn from the widow in 2 Kings 4 is that she took her problem to the prophet. She didn't go to the bank. She didn't go to the credit union. She didn't go get a payday loan. No, she made the connection between her bills and her Bible. She saw the connection between God and gold. That's why she took her problem to the prophet. In other words, she sought a spiritual solution to a physical need. She needed God to intervene in her circumstances and so she sought His way over her way.

I am aware that much of what I preach, teach, and write on overcoming financial hardships in life runs smack-dab into mental roadblocks. It's difficult to do a U-turn when the road is closed. The reason why so many of us stay stuck going in the wrong direction in our lives financially is because we have been so culturally duped about how we are to live. Society has painted a magnificent portrait of self-sufficiency and self-indulgence. It has become normal to live in debt, over your standard of income. And since it has become normal, we no longer see it is as the glaring problem it truly is. We don't recognize the negative consequences that show up in our health, peace, or decisions.

It's difficult to solve something when you are not aware there is anything to solve.

But for those of you who are aware and who want to reverse the negative trends in your life financially—as well as all the emotional, physical, spiritual, and relational consequences that have come about—God has the answer in His Word. He has the answer for us so clearly because God desires for you and me to live successfully in this area of our lives. In fact, He has told us that He will reward us when we do. The wiser we steward the financial resources He's given to us, the more He says He'll give. The reverse of that is true as well. We discover both this blessing and this warning in Luke 16 where Jesus says:

"Whoever is faithful in very little is also faithful in much, and whoever is unrighteous in very little is also unrighteous in much. So if you have not been faithful with worldly wealth, who will trust you with what is genuine? And if you have not been faithful with what belongs to someone else, who will give you what is your own?" (vv. 10–12)

When you are faithful to steward that which God has given to you, He says He will give more. This passage relates to more than just money, but the principle transcends. The problem today is that far too many of us have not been faithful to steward our time, talents, and particularly our treasures with wisdom. So when we pray to God to give us more, He responds by directing us to His Word, which explains that we need to be far more responsible with what we have before expecting more.

To help you steward your finances wisely, and to reverse the negative results of poor money-management, I want to give you three words of advice. It may seem simple to you. It may seem small. Especially if you are staring at a mountain of debt. But if you will apply these three words and seek to honor God with your finances, He will lead you on the path to greater financial freedom as well. Do what you can with what you have right where you are. Start now, and here's how: give, save, and spend. If you will begin to fully apply these three words, in this order, to your financial choices, you will begin to see your financial life turn around. Your path to financial freedom is completely tied to these three words.

The first word touches on the foundation upon which all else is built, since it establishes your recognition of God as your Source. Unfortunately, in Christian circles today we are experiencing a condition that I call "Cirrhosis of the Giver." While American Christians control more than 70 percent of the world's Christian wealth, the average American Christian only gives about 2.5 percent of his or her income.[1] It is estimated that less than 20 percent of all Christians faithfully tithe. And we wonder why we are experiencing so much by way of financial struggles, strain, and defeat. We've failed to put first things first.

> *Your path to financial freedom is completely tied to these three words: give, save, spend.*

When we fail to live out God's principles with regard to stewardship, and in particular giving, we fail to reap God's blessings with regard to reward and provision. We also leave the church short of the kingdom resources necessary to have the kingdom impact God expects His people to make in the world. You can't be a spiritual thief and simultaneously expect the blessings of God.

The reward of financial freedom involves honoring God with your finances (Prov. 3:9–10). If you skip that basic premise, it won't matter what else you do. God has scissors and your pockets will have holes (Hag. 1:6). I was twenty-two years old when I learned this principle. At the time, all I made was $350 a month. We weren't just poor, we were "po!" Yet even though all I made was

$350 a month, before we did anything else at all, a tithe of $35 of it was given to God, as well as an offering of $15 on top of it. In giving the tithe and offering to God, I wasn't just telling Him that I was giving Him my money, I was confessing that I knew He is the owner and I am the steward, and that all I have is His.

It is such a simple principle that it amazes me how many people don't believe it, operate by it, or benefit from it. God didn't make the road to financial U-turns and ultimate victory a mystery. He set up a signpost, clearly marked, and said, "Give to Me, then I will protect, provide for, and promote what you do."

The first step to the reward of financial freedom is to give. The next step is to save.

The second step on the path to experiencing the reward of financial freedom involves an equally unfamiliar word in many circles today: save. Savings is the opposite of debt because savings is future-oriented while debt is past-oriented. Savings involves putting away something for tomorrow, while debt involves paying for yesterday. Unfortunately, around 40 percent of Americans do not have enough savings to cover a $400 emergency.

In fact, biblical principles on money include not only saving for yourself but also saving for your descendants. We read: "A good man leaves an inheritance to his grandchildren . . ." (Prov. 13:22). You aren't merely to be thinking of yourself with regard to your financial plans, you are to be making plans for your grandchildren as well.

Yet most Christians today can't even get around to the grand-children because they haven't gotten around to the children, and worse yet, they haven't gotten around to saving for themselves. The majority of believers are one crisis away from bankruptcy.

The greatest biblical illustration of the benefits of saving comes from the life of Joseph. The principles Joseph followed while in Egypt not only blessed him, they also blessed his family and blessed entire nations. When Pharaoh suffered during a dream that he could not understand, which included seven fat cows and seven lean cows as well as seven good ears of corn and seven scarce ears of corn, Joseph gave us one of the greatest precepts for financial victory we could ever follow. Joseph instructed Pharaoh to take from the abundance and save it so that when the time came for Egypt and the surrounding nations to experience lack, they would have a surplus to fall back on. Scripture tells us Joseph's instructions:

"Let Pharaoh do this: Let him appoint overseers over the land and take a fifth of the harvest of the land of Egypt during the seven years of abundance. Let them gather all the excess food during these good years that are coming. Under Pharaoh's authority, store the grain in the cities, so they may preserve it as food. The food will be a reserve for the land during the seven years of famine that will take place in the land of Egypt. Then the country will not be wiped out by the famine." (Gen. 41:34–36)

Joseph advised Pharaoh to set aside and save during the years of plenty so that there would be plenty to supply everyone's needs in the years of famine. You never know when you are going to run into a month, year, or even a decade of famine. Many people were caught off guard when our nation's economy took a downturn a decade ago. Similarly, we were all surprised by the recent Coronavirus and the economic fallout that ensued. If you have not learned the principle of living a life of financial victory that includes saving for the future, it's hard to survive in times like these.

Both tithing and saving should be an automatic that you take off of the top of your earnings with no questions asked. Even if you have to start out only saving a small amount, you still need to do it. You need to begin to develop the habit of saving. Cultivate the virtue of saying no to instant gratification and yes to prolonged stability.

Many of us are not saving money because we have maxed out our personal budgets. We don't see any surplus to set aside for later because every dollar that comes in is already claimed for something. Our house note, car note, grocery bill, and entertainment bill, along with student loans and credit card debt, make full use of what we earn.

However, there are a few practical tips that can help you cut back on your expenses in an effort to save money. While these do not include all of the money-saving tips that can put you in a better position to be able to save, these are what I call my top nine tips to reduce expenses and manage your money in order to free you up to save so that you can become a better, wiser kingdom steward of your financial resources:

1. **Pay off your debt starting with the smallest bill first.** I know it is easier said than done, but a lot of money these days is going to pay interest on credit cards, thus making it difficult for people to save. There are several strategies to paying off credit card debt. The first involves checking with your lender or lenders concerning whether they can give you a lower interest rate if you close the account and plan to pay it off. Another way is to consolidate your credit card debt into one loan that gives you a lower interest rate. Credit card interest rates can run upwards of 20–30 percent, and it is often possible to get a consolidated loan in order to transfer your debt and have more of your monthly payment going to principle and not to interest.

2. **Cut back on entertainment bills.** Particularly with the invention of cheap or even free ways to view entertainment through online streaming, people do not need to spend so much money each month on a large cable subscription. A lot of what you want to view these days can be accessed through the internet or through inexpensive rental or subscription plans. In addition, wisely choose what time you go to the movies. Matinees at a theater will offer you the same viewing experience for oftentimes less than half the price of an evening show. (And don't blow your savings on

overpriced popcorn or soda. Eat before you go so you won't be tempted to buy.)

3. **Use cash.** Rarely these days do you see anyone paying with cash, but using cash as your primary method of payment gives you a way of seeing how much you really have. Once you have a budget, take out how much you have allocated for food, gas, or anything else that you plan to buy and set aside the cash for purchases. This way you will have a more accurate reading on how much you have to spend, and will be unable to spend more than you budgeted. When the cash is gone for the month, so is the spending. It will only take one or two months of running out early for you to learn principles of spending that will help you not to run out in the future!

4. **Pay off your car or your home early.** You can save a tremendous amount of money simply by making additional payments on any car or home loan that will be applied strictly to the principal on the loan. Once your car or home is paid off, use the extra that you save to invest in your future.

5. **In addition to paying off your car, choose your car wisely.** At the time of this writing, gas prices are painfully high. Choosing a car that conserves gas rather than wastes it is an optimal choice. Yet whatever car you drive can use less gas simply by how you drive it. Using cruise control

while on the highways as well as accelerating slowly rather than quickly can economize the usage of your fuel.

6. **Cook at home and eat leftovers.** Americans spend roughly a little over a third of their annual food budget on eating out. Not only is eating out frequently a poor choice in the types of processed foods that you have to choose from for your health, it is also a poor choice for your wallet if you are battling debt. Consider spending more time planning your grocery list, grocery shopping (when you are not hungry), cooking, and also eating leftovers.

7. **Develop a short-term savings of three to six months' essential living expenses for the quick availability of cash to address emergency needs, and a long-term savings to address retirement and legacy.**

8. **Shop around to make sure that you have the absolutely lowest insurance premium on your home, car, health, or any other insurance you have.** Insurance companies are fairly competitive and will often beat another company's price simply to get your business.

9. **Lose weight God's way.** Americans spend over $40 billion annually on weight-loss products, equipment, memberships, or surgeries. It is one of the top moneymakers in existence. And yet we wouldn't need to lose weight if we followed the biblical principles of taking care of our bodies as the temple of the Holy Spirit, or not giving into behaviors of greed, excess, and gluttony. The basics of

losing weight typically involve self-control and discipline. Limiting simple carbohydrate and sugar intake while balancing your diet with healthy complex carbs, proteins, and fats and consistently exercising won't cost much and will produce steady and long-term results. Walking outside for thirty minutes is free or driving to a nearby park only costs the gas that is used as compared to a membership at a local gym.

There are multiple strategies that you can employ in order to cut back on your expenses in an effort to redirect those funds either to paying down your debt, or to saving. These are just a few. Yet whatever you do, begin the process of saving now. Even if it's just to get you used to the concept until you are able to save a larger portion of your income each month, start now.

The third area that you should focus on regarding your finances is how you spend. Once you have given to God the tithe and, as you are able, the offerings, and once you have used a portion of your money for savings, the remainder of what you have is yours to spend. But don't go spend it on anything and everything. The Bible has principles related to your spending habits as well. The first one I want to touch on again briefly is your budget. You need a budget. Without a budget, you will not be able to make the most of your money, and you will run the risk of spending more than you have. As we saw earlier in this chapter, God is in the planning business. He wants to bless a plan.

We read in Proverbs: "Commit your activities to the LORD, and your plans will be established" (16:3). I am amazed at the number of families whom I counsel who do not have a financial plan. Every Christian family should have a plan for how they expect to spend the resources God has given them. If there is no plan, then there is nothing to ask God to help out with.

If you do not have a financial plan or a budget for where your money will go, you need to make one now. If you already have one, make sure it lines up with the fol-lowing principles. Because if you will practice and live by these pre-cepts, you will live in financial vic-tory. That is not to say you will be a millionaire, but it is to say that you will have the capacity to enjoy and maximize the financial blessings and resources God has given you.

Without a budget, you will not be able to make the most of your money, and you will run the risk of spending more than you have.

Make sure that your needs come before your wants, or you may end up losing your needs at the expense of your wants. And leave room in your budget for helping others. The greatest command is to love God with all of your heart. The second greatest command is to love others. If God has blessed you with financial gain in any way, it is so He can use it to be a blessing to others as well. Remember, the definition of a blessing is being able to enjoy and extend the favor of God in your life. If it stops with you, it is an incomplete blessing.

God blesses in order for you to bless. Plan to bless. Leave room in your budget for ways to help. You will be amazed at how great it feels to be able to assist someone in need. We read in Acts 20:

> "In every way I've shown you that it is necessary to help the weak by laboring like this and to remember the words of the Lord Jesus, because he said, 'It is more blessed to give than to receive.'" (v. 35)

Invest in others with the resources God has given you, and you will be blessed. It is a guarantee. Give, save, learn how to be content with what you have (Heb. 13:5), use your money wisely, and plan a budget for what you receive, and you will be walking on the path to financial victory.

Remember, there is nothing wrong with having things unless you can't pay your bills and the money that God has given you is going to interest on accumulated debt. That is when it is time to see what you can sell in order to pay what you owe. You must make the decision now to start living within your means, avoiding unnecessary borrowing, and developing a short- and long-term financial plan. Give God something specific to respond to.

Invest in others with the resources God has given you, and you will be blessed.

The widow in financial distress that we looked at earlier in 2 Kings 4 was given a unique instruction from the prophet on how to make a profit and get out of debt. God has a million ways of providing for you. When you align yourself under Him, He will give you the direction you need to turn your financial setbacks around. This is what He did with the widow in dire need of some income. When she went to the prophet, he then told her a very interesting business plan. He said that she should go to her neighbors and ask them to give her all of the empty pots that they had in their houses. He told her to take anything her neighbors had to spare, and then pour what was left of her oil in them.

The problem was that this lady had very little oil to pour. She could have easily told the prophet that his solution didn't make sense. But in faith, she trusted God instead. After gathering the empty pots, the single woman went into her home and closed the door and began to pour what little oil she possessed. As she began to pour, she saw that the oil did not run out.

All she had was a little, but God took her little when she responded in faith and created much. We read that the woman, "said to her son, 'Bring me another container.' But he replied, 'There aren't any more.' Then the oil stopped. She went and told the man of God, and he said, 'Go sell the oil and pay your debt; you and your sons can live on the rest'" (2 Kings 4:6–7).

The prophet had given the woman the insight and guidance she needed to tap into God's overwhelming supply. He had given her a divinely inspired business approach. She would not have known it had she not sought him out and followed what he said. No one could have come up with such a seemingly impossible way for her to pay off her debt, except for the prophet who knew it would work.

Similarly, God has a plan for you. And, to be honest, it is probably not a plan you could think of on your own. This widow would have never come up with the business strategy of the prophet on her own. God's will is what works. Not our own strategies. In order to tap into His will, you need to align yourself closely with Him through the power of His Spirit.

Far too many conferences, books, and "life coaches" seek to sell people strategies for personal gain based on logic or best practices that work for some and don't work for others (usually they work for the ones selling it only!). But God doesn't need you to read another book, go to another seminar, or hire a life coach when He has given you the solution already. Align your heart, thoughts, words, and actions under His overarching rule, and you will be so close to Him that you will hear His direction when He guides you. You will know what to do that will return a profit. You will catch the break, find the favor, or discover just how to make oil stretch a lot further than it ever could on your own.

If you are struggling with the pain of negative financial consequences in your life today and you will take the time and the effort to seek God, He will meet you where you are. He reversed the tragic situation of the widow about to lose her two children, and He can certainly reverse anything you are facing right now as well.

No, I can't tell you the exact details of God's unique financial plan for you because His ways are higher than our ways and

His thoughts are higher than our thoughts (Isa. 55:9). Beyond that even, God's specific plan varies from person to person. But what I can tell you is that if you will put Him and His principles first in your life, He will show you His plan for you. He will put a thought in your mind that you never had before, or bring some concept to you that shows you how to turn your financial losses into financial gains.

God has a way of cancelling out our debts and turning us around. But you will never discover His plan for you until you seek Him first: "But seek first the kingdom of God and his righteousness, and all these things will be provided for you" (Matt. 6:33). That's a promise—a promise you can take all the way to the bank.

CHAPTER ELEVEN

Reversing Sexual Consequences

 In cultural traditions, it is told that the Eskimos had a very interesting way of killing wolves. One of the ways they would do so was to take a knife and stick it in ice with the blade pointed up. Then they would coat the icy blade with blood, knowing that the scent of the blood would draw in the wolves. The result would be a wolf smelling the scent of blood. Because the blood was frozen on the knife, the wolf would lick the knife. Of course, because the temperature was so cold, the wolf wouldn't necessarily feel its own tongue as it began to be cut by the blade of the knife.

All the wolf would focus on was the blood on the knife, even as that blood began to be mixed with its own. After a while, the wolf would bleed to death, not even knowing it was the cause of its own demise. Entrapped by the enjoyment of licking the bloody knife, the wolf would be tricked into its own destruction.

This is a great metaphor for sexual immorality.

Many people have fallen prey to their own pleasures, leading to spiritual death. The Bible is replete with information on the consequences that come through illicit sexual behavior. Lives are shattered, legacies dismantled, and dreams aborted through this one kind of sin—more so than through any other. Sexual immorality has ushered the devolution of humanity and the resultant consequences of that devolution are on par with nothing else. There is most likely not one person reading this book who has not experienced the negative ramifications of immoral sexual relations, thoughts, or behaviors—either through their own choices or through someone they love who has brought those consequences to them.

Yet despite the known disastrous results of sexual immorality, our culture promotes it like it is the best thing since sliced bread. We are a sex-saturated society. The internet, television, music, conversations, and books all give us access to, and a hearty approval for, this particular sin. It has become the drug of choice within the culture, making promiscuity (and all thoughts and actions tied to it) the number-one destroying force for finances, families, and futures. There used to be shame associated with illicit sex or sexually deviant choices. There used to be shame connected to the misuse of humanity, particularly women, in pornography. But now it's become like a fast-food drive-thru for so many people. It's just part of life, despite the myriads of studies that demonstrate a connection between illicit sex, immoral behavior, and pornographic use with a lack of ability to connect relationally to others or even to perform at an optimum level sexually.

Sexual sin is wreaking havoc on our nation and world. Not just by what it does to the human psyche and the resulting negative impact on true intimacy, but also by what it does to life. Unwanted and unplanned pregnancies have created an entire industry that supports the killing of children in the womb. The high cost of this killing spree adds up not only in the sheer millions of lives lost annually, but also in the emotional, spiritual, physical, and psychological consequences left on the mother, and often on the father as well.

In addition to this, diseases have also run rampant due to sexual immorality. Sexually transmitted diseases now come in all shapes and sizes, giving rise to a pharmaceutical industry aimed strictly at combating, curing, or controlling these viruses and diseases.

The plethora of mechanisms at work in society that gives license and liberty to all manner of sexual immorality has ushered us into a new era where sexuality is defined by choice. In 2014, Facebook offered its users fifty-eight different genders to choose from.[2] Obviously, they were behind the times, because at the time of this writing, more than 110 different variations on gender identity exist as options for the general public. Keep in mind, a person is not tied to remain as any of those 110 (or more—whose counting?) variations for any length of time. You can choose to be one gender around breakfast and another in the evening. Children as young as grade school are now being given the option to cross-dress or receive hormone-inhibiting drugs to limit their development in their God-given gender of male or female.

And while you may identify as the male or female that God made you, and you may also be attracted to the opposite sex, as God intended, you might still struggle with other sexual issues or consequences. Sexual sins have cost many a couple their marriage and family. It's cost many others their reputations. Some have had to change careers or even move. Others have had to change churches, or be let go from churches where they once served.

The generations of single-parent families that are now caught in a cycle of grandmothers raising children as the single mother works two or three jobs has taken its toll on the overall health and harmony of most homes.

And while your own sexual history may not have produced such grievous consequences as some I have listed, most of us can look back and say with regret, "I wish I hadn't done that." There are many more who have a history of having been used, abused, and thrown away when the playtime had ended. They carry scars of other people's lust for power, pleasure, and control. So, my purpose in this chapter is to seek to approach this very sensitive topic of sexual sin and its consequences from a bibliocentric worldview that aims to promote healing. No matter where you are on the continuum, I hope you become part of the process of spiritual recovery through our time on this subject.

Sex was created by heaven, not Hollywood. It was God's idea, and the Bible tells us that God saw His creation and called it "good" (Gen. 1:31). Sex is good. In the context within which we are to experience it, sex is very good.

But Satan is an expert at taking what has been created by God for good and perverting it into something very bad. In fact, Satan's first attempt at breeding destruction into the sexual act came when demons inhabited men and then had relations with women. They then gave birth to hybrids who incarnated in all manner of wickedness. Satan uses sexual immorality to expand his kingdom. As a result, the earth had to be flooded in order to rid the land of the corrupted life that had taken residence on it (Gen. 6:1–7).

Ever since then, Satan has not relented nor slowed down on his attempts to infiltrate and infect humanity through sexual sins. The problem with this particular area of sin is that it is the most natural focus in our lives. Sex is born out of a natural God-given desire. It's not a sin we need to look outwardly to locate. No, this sin comes tied to that which is already legitimately built within us. It's situated within our human DNA. But like saltwater, when you drink it to satisfy your thirst, it can eventually kill you.

> *Satan is an expert at taking what has been created by God for good and perverting it into something very bad.*

Our desire for sexual intimacy is rooted in our spiritual connection to God's covenant. Initially, sexual relations serve as a way to both inaugurate and set in motion the marriage covenant. The covenant of marriage is both sealed and confirmed by the first marital sexual encounter.

Yet what the culture has done is take something that was given to us as an enjoyable gift for marriage and has removed the covenant aspect of the action. When the purpose for the activity is removed, the activity itself becomes meaningless and without boundaries.

In a fireplace, a fire is a beautiful thing. It warms the room. But when the sparks fly and are allowed to go anywhere and everywhere in a home, it will burn down the entire house. God created a fireplace for sex, and He called it marriage. But we have allowed the sparks of sex to go outside of the fireplace. As a result, we are experiencing a destructive burning in our lives, relationships, and world.

Scripture addresses a whole plethora of sexual deviations in Leviticus 18. This chapter covers areas such as fornication, adultery, homosexuality, incest, bestiality, and more. It goes over all the ways in which humanity has removed the intent of sexual relations away from God's design. The entirety of Proverbs 5 warns against adultery, outlining the damage that it does. In Job 31:9–12, we read about the realm of destruction sexual immorality brings to yourself and others. And Paul says in 1 Thessalonians 4:1–8 that the proof that you are growing spiritually is when you are controlling sexual desire and it is no longer controlling you. The reverse of that is true as well. Paul calls this a test of sanctification. You know how much you are spiritually progressing by how well you are able to manage your sexual desires.

Paul gives an extended discussion of this in 1 Corinthians 6:9 where he comes down boldly and harshly against those who practice a lifestyle of sexual sin. He says: "Don't you know that the unrighteous will not inherit God's kingdom? Do not be deceived: No sexually immoral people, idolaters, adulterers, or males who have sex with males . . ." Paul clearly outlines how this lifestyle blocks a person from inheriting the manifestation of the kingdom of God.

Now, don't misunderstand this to say that a person cannot enter eternal life through faith in Jesus Christ for the forgiveness of sins. You enter heaven based on your faith in the finished work of Jesus Christ. But you inherit the manifestation of the kingdom of God, accruing the benefits of the kingdom, based on what you do or don't do. So, while someone may be on his or her way to heaven, heaven may not be on its way to them when they choose to live a sexually immoral lifestyle. Sexual immorality can block God's working of favor and blessing in your life. Consequences don't always show up as something decidedly negative like a health issue of some sort. No, consequences often manifest as the removal or discontinuance of blessings and favor that were once yours. This makes it much harder to identify but not any less impactful.

So as you examine this area of your life in particular, keep your mind and your heart open for God to reveal to you areas where you either need to repent of past doings, forgive those who have wronged you, or repent and change course in present doings—or all of the above. Ask God to bring to your mind areas where you need to get right with Him regarding sexual misconduct, if even it were only in the heart. As Jesus said:

> "You have heard that it was said, 'Do not commit adultery.' But I tell you, everyone who looks at a woman lustfully has already committed adultery with her in his heart." (Matt. 5:27–28)

In today's sexually saturated social media culture that verse undoubtedly applies to both men and women. Sexual sin is more prevalent than most of us probably even realize. Because it is, we need to face it directly in stopping the source of sin in our own lives and reversing any consequences that need addressed.

Paul gave us insight into how to approach sexual temptation when he wrote in what is one of the greatest books at living a life of purity ever written:

> "Everything is permissible for me," but not everything is beneficial. "Everything is permissible for me," but I will not be mastered by anything. "Food is for the stomach and the stomach for food," and God will do away with both of them. However, the body is not for sexual immorality but for the Lord, and the Lord for the body. God raised

up the Lord and will also raise us up by his power. (1 Cor. 6:12–14)

Paul takes the subject of sex deep theologically when he starts out by saying that all things may be lawful, but all things are not beneficial (profitable). The root of the desire may be natural, but the way you are expressing it is not. Whenever anything holds you hostage, it is spiritually unlawful. Paul reminds us that we are not to be mastered by anything other than the Lord Jesus Christ. If and when we are controlled by our passions, we are being ruled and will face the consequences of that rebellion away from God's rule.

Paul explains in this passage that while food is for the stomach, your body is for the Lord. There is a difference. Your body is not yours to do whatever you want with. God has not only raised the Lord up but will also raise each of us up if we have placed our faith in Christ, through His power. In other words, Christ lives within us. We are to be one with Him in all we do. Paul continues in this passage by explaining:

> Don't you know that your bodies are a part of Christ's body? So should I take a part of Christ's body and make it part of a prostitute? Absolutely not! Don't you know that anyone joined to a prostitute is one body with her? For Scripture says, "The two will become one flesh." But anyone joined to the Lord is one spirit with him.
>
> Flee sexual immorality! Every other sin a person commits is outside the body, but the person who is sexually

immoral sins against his own body. Don't you know that your body is a temple of the Holy Spirit who is in you, whom you have from God? You are not your own, for you were bought at a price. So glorify God with your body. (1 Cor. 6:15–20)

When you have sex (whether physically, virtually, or in your mind), you enter into a union. As a believer, though, you are already in a union. You are one in Spirit with Jesus Christ. Wherever you go, He goes. Whatever you do, He does. Thus, when you enter into an immoral sexual activity, you are literally asking Jesus to become an active participant in it with you—which, due to His holiness, He cannot do. Thus, you sever yourself from the presence and power of grace in your life that comes through an abiding with Christ (John 15).

You are to flee immorality because this particular sin is a sin against your own self in every way. This is a unique sin that brings with it a unique set of circumstances and consequences producing internal damage to the core of who you are.

If you get chewing gum or melted wax on the carpet and try to remove it, you're going to have to take some of the carpet with it. This is because the gum or the dried wax has intertwined with the fibers of the carpet. To get the gunk out of the carpet will require removing some of the carpet too. When you enter into a sexual union, you are becoming intertwined with the object of your engagement. Thus, when you seek to disconnect from it at a later time, you have to leave some of yourself behind. It leaves a scar on the soul, torn apart through sexual entanglements.

Your body is the temple of the living God. A temple is a house of worship. Your emotions, spirit, and body were designed in such a way as to offer the Creator of the Universe worship. But when you use your body in any way other than what God has prescribed, you are entering into false worship and, therefore, limiting your ability to be who you were designed to be. You are to glorify God with your body, not dishonor Him with it.

All of that sounds good and we believe it. But the reality of life is that most of us have already gotten so far down this road of sexual immorality—at one point in our lives, if not more—that we are paying the piper even now. We've been through things, done things, looked at things, thought of things, and have denigrated ourselves to such a degree that we're paying the price. If stories were told by readers of this book, most would be full of regrets, mistakes, sins, failures, and shame. So how do we do a U-turn from the negative consequences of sexual sins? Jesus gives us the pathway in John 8.

In this passage, we read about the account of the woman caught in adultery. The Pharisees had sought to trick Jesus in order that they might accuse Him. They attempted to put Him in a catch-22 in order that whatever answer He gave would be a losing answer. This is because if He told them to stone the woman caught in adultery, He would be disagreeing with the law of Rome, which did not allow for capital punishment. But if He said not to stone her, He would be disagreeing with the law of Moses.

Yet Jesus' answer took Him out of a no-win situation because He chose to answer them in an entirely different way. Rather than casting judgment or release through His words, He simply bent down and started writing in the sand. The exact words that He wrote are not given to us in the passage, but we do know what transpired both during and after He wrote. We read:

> Jesus stooped down and starting writing on the ground with his finger. When they persisted in questioning him, he stood up and said to them, "The one without sin among you should be the first to throw a stone at her." Then he stooped down again and continued writing on the ground. When they heard this, they left one by one, starting with the older men. Only he was left, with the woman in the center. (John 8:6b–9)

When He wrote the second time, the men began to drop their stones and walk away. In using His finger to write twice in the dirt, Jesus was bringing forth an allusion to the content of the two tablets of the Law of Moses that God wrote with His finger; it may have been these very commands He was writing. Thus, Jesus was declaring Himself the author of the Law while simultaneously revealing that they, too, had broken God's law and, therefore, stood condemned. It emptied the town until Jesus was left alone with the woman. Jesus didn't deny the fact that there was sin. Rather, He dealt with the reality of illegitimate judgment by others on that sin. After the people left, Jesus told the woman that He did not condemn her either. He also told her to "go, and . . . sin no more" (John 8:11 ESV). He set her free with the command to honor her freedom with personal purity.

Jesus didn't say go and sin no more, and then I won't condemn you. That is what we often do. We wait for someone, or even ourselves, to demonstrate moral purity before we will stop judging. But Jesus said the reverse. He removed any hint of condemnation and then out of the grace of that gift, the woman was to live a life of honor. That same release that He gave to the woman is also available to you right now. In fact, we read about it in Romans 8:1 (NASB) where it says, "Therefore, there is now no condemnation for those who are in Christ Jesus." The consequences for sexual sin have been reversed at the cross of Jesus Christ. Unfortunately, far too many of us condemn ourselves or others to such a degree that we elongate the consequences or deepen their cuts by living in a state of shame, guilt, or blame.

But, in Christ, condemnation has gone. Along with that is shame, guilt, and blame as well. They are not of Christ. We are to allow the grace of Jesus to motivate us to live a life of holiness. Now, grace does not mean you are to cover up sin as you continue to do it. You are not to continue in sin in any way. But when you choose to repent and turn from sin, Jesus is there to help you to your feet and send you on the right path of moral purity.

The consequences for sexual sin have been reversed at the cross of Jesus Christ.

Grace is to be our mentor and teacher. We read about it this way in Titus 2:11–13:

> For the grace of God has appeared, bringing salvation for all people, instructing us to deny godlessness and worldly lusts and to live in a sensible, righteous, and godly way in the present age, while we wait for the blessed hope, the appearing of the glory of our great God and Savior, Jesus Christ.

Let grace guide you. Choosing to remain in a state of shame, guilt, regret, bitterness, or any of the sort related to sexual immorality will only compound the consequences by adding more of the same. Sexual immorality is just the first snowball that creates an avalanche of negative demise in a person's life due to the emotional, spiritual, and physical response to the sin. But when you allow yourself to forgive yourself, or forgive someone else who may have mistreated you, or forgive your parents who may have divorced due to sexual sin, or whatever the case may be—you let go of condemnation. Letting go of condemnation allows you to grab ahold of grace. It is grace that will enable you to deny future ungodliness and worldly desires and to live sensibly. It is grace that can set you on the right path of hope, peace, and love.

If you've already blown it and need help to heal, pray this prayer:

> *"Lord Jesus, I recognize You are here in my life and I want the grace and mercy that will allow me to move forward. I can't*

change yesterday, but I repent of my sexual sins and ask You for forgiveness. I forgive myself and those who have hurt me. I'm here today and I want a better tomorrow. Thank You for forgiveness, no condemnation, freedom from guilt, freedom from shame, and for Your grace. Amen."

Most of us send our clothes out to the cleaners when they get dirty. We send them out if there is a stain. The cleaning shop removes the stain using expensive equipment that will make your clothes look like new. The reason why we send our clothes to the cleaners is because we want to wear them again. Similarly, God has His own cleaning system. It's called the atoning blood of Jesus Christ. When you and I come to Him with our sins and receive His cleaning in our lives, we are able to be used by Him again.

A dirty diamond is still a diamond. It just needs to be polished and cleaned in order to experience the full brilliance of its sparkle. You have a purpose. God has created you to live out a brilliant purpose. It's called your destiny. And in living out your destiny, you will shine. But before you can pursue it fully, you need to understand the power of His forgiveness in your life for whatever sin you may have committed. Come to Jesus at the foot of the cross and let go of the guilt, shame, and regret of yesterday. Or, turn from the sin you may be living in today. Instead, receive His grace and pursue tomorrow with a purified passion to live out His kingdom agenda in all that you do. As Jesus said, "Go, and . . . sin no more" (John 8:11 esv).

CHAPTER TWELVE

Reversing Irreversible Consequences

One of the most important passages of Scripture is Isaiah 55:8–9. This chapter speaks to the importance of returning to God so that God will have compassion on us. It urges us to seek the Lord and find Him, to call on Him and know that He is near. But, perhaps even more important than that, this passage reminds us who we are and who God is. We are finite; God is infinite. We see through a mirror dimly. God sees past, present, and future simultaneously. We comprehend little; God comprehends all. We think we know the way; God really knows the way.

The reason why these principles are important is because we can forfeit our own destiny in our future by refusing to follow

God's leading in our lives. We think we know how to accomplish x, y, or z, so we pursue our own path, only to discover we've gone miles upon miles in the wrong direction. Not only do we then need a U-turn, but we have lost time on the journey back to where we should have gone in the first place.

Isaiah 55:8–9 succinctly sums up this foundational truth for each of us when it says:

"For my thoughts are not your thoughts, and your ways are not my ways." This is the LORD's declaration. "For as heaven is higher than earth, so my ways are higher than your ways, and my thoughts than your thoughts."

God sees all. God knows all. God understands all. Because of this, His ways and His thoughts are not on the same level as ours.

We think we know the way; God really knows the way.

His direction and guidance in our lives may sound strange. We may question why He allows what He does. We may scratch our heads and try to figure out His plan. But, in the end, this passage reminds us that we may never figure out His plan on this side of heaven. His perspective is simply too much higher, broader, wiser, grander, and transcending than ours.

That's why faith is so critical in a believer's life. Faith demonstrates through our actions that we trust God even when we don't understand Him.

No biblical account demonstrates this more than the healing of a man named Naaman. We are introduced to Naaman in 2 Kings 5:1 (NASB) when we read: "Now Naaman, captain of the army of the king of Aram, was a great man with his master, and highly respected, because by him the LORD had given victory to Aram. The man was also a valiant warrior . . ." Naaman had it going on. He was respected, valued, and deserving of honor. The Scripture tells us he was not only a captain of an army for the king but that he had the reputation of being a great man.

In fact, people weren't the only ones who valued Naaman. The passage tells us that God esteemed him as well, and showed that through what He chose to do through him. The Lord had given the victory to the king through Naaman's command and leading of the army.

No doubt Naaman's name was great throughout the land of his friends and the land of his enemies. Had he lived today, he would probably have millions of followers on social media. People had placed their confidence in him and, over time, he had demonstrated his ability to retain it. That's no small thing in light of the fickle nature of humanity.

But the passage we read earlier told us one more thing about Naaman that I have not yet mentioned. After saying that he was "a valiant warrior," we read a very telling term: *But*. Accolade after accolade is listed about this man, yet the attention of most readers will become piqued at the one small conjunction following it all: *But*.

Naaman had all of the respect a man could muster, *but* . . .

Naaman had prestige and honor, *but* . . .

Naaman knew victory through his leadership, *but* . . .

The four words following this word *but* would change everything. Because we learn that despite all of his accomplishments, wealth, and skills, "he was a leper."

In that day and age, leprosy meant more than just disease. It meant a cessation of work. It meant isolation from others through a quarantined lifestyle. It meant the loss of personal identity, fellowship, and funds. Leprosy did more than strip the health of a person through the disease; it also stripped away their dignity. It's one thing to be unwell. It's another to be unwell and helpless, while simultaneously removed from those who could or would give help.

As leprosy spreads, lesions and sores tear through the skin and bring about excruciating levels of pain. Deformity was the only thing to look ahead to, prior to death. This incurable disease offered no hope. Even hospice wasn't an option because no one else wanted to go around someone with leprosy. The diagnosis of leprosy was a death sentence without dignity. And despite Naaman's awards, plaques, accomplishments, victories, and recognition, the knock of death on his door reminded him he was just human after all. He had become both a conqueror and a castaway.

Yet because of Naaman's past achievements and notoriety, there were many who wanted to help him as best that they could. He wasn't rejected like so many who found themselves in his situation.

One of the people who wanted to help him was a young girl who served in his home. She saw his distress and knew what would eventually come from the disease, and she remembered the prophet from where she had been captured. In her homeland of Israel lived a prophet named Elisha. He could do miracles, and he could surely cure Naaman, this girl assumed. So she urged them to go to Israel. We read:

> Now the Arameans had gone out in bands and had taken captive a little girl from the land of Israel; and she waited on Naaman's wife. She said to her mistress, "I wish that my master were with the prophet who is in Samaria! Then he would cure him of his leprosy." Naaman went in and told his master, saying, "Thus and thus spoke the girl who is from the land of Israel." (2 Kings 5:2–4 NASB)

Naaman and his wife liked this idea. They had run out of their own options. They knew there was no cure. The doctors had given up on them. But this young girl who served in their home sparked hope. She suggested a solution. And even though the solution was far away and a little strange, they jumped at the option. So, Naaman went to his boss for permission and supplies to go see the prophet.

Like I said, the girl's solution wasn't normal. It didn't make sense. It wasn't a thought grasped by most. That's why Naaman's boss missed it altogether. He didn't even hear what Naaman said. Or, if he did, he chose to interpret it differently according to his own logic and knowledge. Going to Israel made sense. But why go to an unknown, obscure prophet who probably lived hand-to-mouth himself? That didn't make sense at all.

So the king drafted a letter to someone much more powerful. He decided to leverage his own power to help Naaman. He wrote to the king of Israel and asked for his direct help.

Now, favors don't come without a cost for royalty, so the king of Aram also included ten talents of silver and six thousand shekels of gold, among other things (2 Kings 5:5). In today's economy, that would be equivalent to over a million dollars. The king of Aram sought to buy Naaman's solution. He thought enough money, enough resources, and enough friendly pressure from a neighboring kingdom would give him what he wanted: Naaman's healing.

But there's one thing physical sickness will teach anyone real quick—no matter your money, connections, or the leverage you may think you have, God has the final say when it comes to health. You can't buy yourself a healing. You can't manipulate yourself a healing. You can't even negotiate a healing. Healing comes from the hand of God, and Him alone, when He so chooses.

The king of Aram didn't realize that yet. His position had gotten to his head, so along with the money and pressure, he sent a letter to the king of Israel that said, "I have sent Naaman my servant to you, that you may cure him of his leprosy" (2 Kings 5:6b NASB). Here's the money. Here's my seal. Here's my request. Heal Naaman, oh king.

The thing is, life doesn't work that way, which the king of Aram, as well as Naaman, would quickly find out. The king of Israel didn't take long to respond. Nor did he mince his words. We read:

> When the king of Israel read the letter, he tore his clothes and said, "Am I God, to kill and to make alive, that this man is sending word to me to cure a man of his leprosy? But consider now, and see how he is seeking a quarrel against me." (2 Kings 5:7 NASB)

To put it another way, he said, "No." The king didn't want a battle. He didn't want to be pressured into curing an incurable disease, something he could not do. He didn't want to be tricked into war or humiliation. So he responded quickly and decisively with his refusal to have any part in the situation at all. Health was in God's hands, he reminded everyone through both his words and actions. So bold was the king's response, that word got out concerning him tearing his clothes. When Elisha heard it, he sent word through a messenger to the king in order to have the sick man come to him. He wanted the situation restored. As he said, "Now let him come to me, and he shall know that there is a prophet in Israel" (2 Kings 5:8 NASB).

Elisha had no qualms in asking for the man to come to him. He knew he could cure an incurable disease, should God want him to. This was nothing to him. Naaman should have gone to him first. But, instead, he had gone to where he thought true power resided. He went to the professionals. He went to the government. He went to where the money, research, and expertise was known to be. After all, who goes to a prophet you've never even heard of? Naaman was a successful military commander. He knew power when he saw it.

Or, did he? Because even when the king of Israel sent him to the prophet Elisha, Naaman balked. Maybe *balked* is not a strong enough word. Scripture tells us he became "furious." Why? Because the prophet hadn't bothered to come himself. The prophet didn't play into Naaman's ego. Not only that, but he had also sent the solution via a messenger, and Naaman thought the solution sounded wrong. He thought it sounded like a joke. There was no logic to the solution, so he probably thought the prophet was playing him. As a result, he left his solution in a rage. We read:

> Elisha sent a messenger to him, saying, "Go and wash in the Jordan seven times, and your flesh will be restored to you and you will be clean." But Naaman was furious and went away and said, "Behold, I thought, 'He will surely come out to me and stand and call on the name of the LORD his God, and wave his hand over the place and cure the leper.' Are not Abanah and Pharpar, the rivers of Damascus, better than all the waters of Israel? Could I not wash in them and be clean?" So he turned and went away in a rage. (2 Kings 5:10–12 NASB)

Obviously, Captain Naaman didn't buy the prophet's approach. Not only did he feel insulted due to being spoken to through a messenger, but he also did not agree with the choice of rivers to dip in.

The Jordan was dirty. Didn't this prophet know anything? Naaman didn't think so. That's why he stormed off in a rage. It took more rational men around him to talk him out of leaving altogether.

Verse 13 (NASB) says that his servants sought to speak sense into him. We read, "Then his servants came near and spoke to him and said, 'My father, had the prophet told you to do some great thing, would you not have done it? How much more then, when he says to you, 'Wash, and be clean'?"

It's possible his servants had come from Israel, like the slave girl who had first urged him to go and see the prophet Elisha. It's possible that his servants also knew of Elisha's history and reputation. They had faith when Naaman had none, which is why they encouraged him to at least give it a try. They appealed to his intellect by explaining that it wasn't the prophet he didn't trust, it was the plan. Had the prophet told him to do something great, he would have done it. Naaman just didn't care for the plan. To wash in a dirty river seven times didn't sound like it would work at all. It didn't even give the slightest glimpse of hope. It sounded bad before he even began.

But Naaman hadn't gotten where he was in life through making all of his own decisions. He knew when to listen and take the advice of others who may know more than him. That's what great leaders do. So Naaman followed the advice of his servants and went to the Jordan. He allowed their faith to carry him when he didn't have any of his own.

This is an important lesson for all of us when we are failing in our faith. When we struggle to believe. When we doubt the message and the messenger. When we struggle in despair and just don't know how we will get through another day. Great leaders, and great people, listen to others who may know more than they know. It's okay to lean on someone else's faith when yours is waning. Sometimes others see more clearly than you do because your vision has become blurred by the pain of your present reality. Greatness doesn't always mean knowing the right way to go. Often it means letting those who know the right way to go guide you. Greatness comes wrapped in humility or it is not greatness at all.

Naaman had reached his lowest level. He had no other options, and he knew it. So, in humility, he chose to listen to those around him and head down to the Jordan River in order to do what the prophet had instructed him to do. Naaman dipped seven times in the Jordan River, and his skin became as healthy as it had ever been before (2 Kings 5:14 NASB). The passage describes his skin like, ". . . the flesh of a little child and he was clean."

It is when Naaman let go of his own way that he was freed up to follow God's way. He had to release his own plans and power prior to receiving God's gift of restoration in his life. For Naaman, the Jordan River was a dirty river. But to the prophet Elisha, it was the place where God did miracles. If only Naaman had understood and known that, he may have gone there even sooner. But Naaman was too stuck on his own methods to recognize he couldn't make miracles on his own. No matter how much money, notoriety, or esteem a person may have on this planet, it's God alone who makes miracles. And sometimes God seeks to remind us of this by allowing us to be in situations that no man can fix. He allows our mess to get so bad that man-made solutions no longer exist. He does this so He can demonstrate who alone is God.

Proverbs 14:12 reminds us, "There is a way that seems right to a person, but its end is the way to death." God's solutions aren't always difficult. In fact, they are often so simple that we brush them off in our human wisdom. We think, "Surely it's not that easy," as we go and try something of our own to fix whatever mess we face. But God's solutions and His miracles throughout Scripture often defined themselves as simple. An act of faith. A restored spirit through repentance. Holding up a rod. Putting feet in water. Marching around an enormous wall seven times. Or, even dipping in the muddy Jordan River.

Remember, Isaiah 55:8 told us clearly: "'For my thoughts are not your thoughts, and your ways are not my ways.' This is the LORD's declaration." It didn't say that God's thoughts involve way more complex and difficult solutions. It just said that God's thoughts are different than ours. Far too often we miss our U-turn because we try to complicate things with our own solutions. We try to get our hands in the mix when God already has it planned out. We increase our pain and extend our misery because we refuse to let go and trust that He knows best. All the while God stands there, proverbial hands on hips, thinking, *If only you would just dip. It ain't that deep. Just do as I say, and you'll be clean.*

Never let your pride keep you from accepting the solution to your problem. Go down to the Jordan and dip seven times. Do what God says. You will discover, as Naaman did, that God knows exactly what He is doing.

Now, be careful that you do all of what God says. Had Naaman kept looking at his skin each time he dipped, and if he had been discouraged by the lesions and chose to stop before he reached seven—he wouldn't have been healed. A lot of people want to obey God up to a point, but then get mad at God when He doesn't give them the fullness of what they asked for. Naaman had to dip seven times to receive his healing. He had to obey fully in order to receive fully. Partial obedience is disobedience, and partial obedience will not bring about deliverance.

> *Never let your pride keep you from accepting the solution to your problem.*

As we have traveled through various setbacks and negative consequences in our lives in this book and draw closer to concluding this chapter, I want to emphasize that God's plan for your U-turn may not make sense to you. But a partial U-turn is no U-turn. Keep that in mind. You have to complete the U-turn to go in the other direction. A partial U-turn will just take you off-roading, where things will get even bumpier and potentially disastrous.

Naaman dipped seven times. Whatever God is asking you to do, do it fully. Even if you don't see immediate results. Even if your faith falters before it grows. Even if you doubt the process and mock the prophet who sent it. Obey fully. Do it because God's ways are not your ways and His thoughts are not your thoughts. Do it because you put your trust in Him by faith. You and I must stop arguing with God's Word. His Word is final. We may not like it. We may not prefer it. We may not even understand it. But it is final, settled in heaven.

When a person gets stuck in quicksand, they resort to what comes natural to them. They often flail their arms and try to climb out, but all the while, these actions only make things worse. Quicksand is sand mixed with water. When sand mixes with water, it removes the friction of sand on sand. Without the friction, a person has nothing to push against in order to extract themselves. Like with water, pushing against quicksand only drags you in deeper.

In order to be rescued from quicksand, a person has to shun the natural response and do what comes unnatural to them. They have to fight their human inclinations and instead relax. Relaxing slows down the sinking. Relaxing allows them to paddle gently as if treading water. It gives them time to either have someone toss them a rope or to slowly paddle to more solid ground.

Life can often feel like quicksand. We get sucked into the drama, pain, loss, and demise life seems to bring us. And while our natural inclination is to fight our way out, leveraging all the strength, might, and muscle we have, doing so will only cause us to sink further. God's ways are higher than our ways. His thoughts are higher than our thoughts. In times of struggle, He asks us to let go of our solutions and trust His. He asks us to abide in Him and His Word, aligning our actions under His covenantal rule. He asks for our hearts to simply believe. In the words of Jesus, "Don't let your heart be troubled. Believe in God; believe also in me" (John 14:1).

Your U-turn happens right there, in your heart. Do not let your heart be troubled. Yes, life brings pain. It comes with disappointments. It carries consequences due to your own behaviors and the actions of others. But Jesus says clearly, "Don't let your heart be troubled. Believe . . ."

Believe.

I emphasized earlier in the book the starting point for reversing the negative consequences in your life. It involved the process of repentance. Repenting of what you did wrong and/or repenting of a wrong response (bitterness, blame, shame, hatred, self-hatred, etc.) toward what others have done wrong to you. Then, when you repented, you were to receive God's forgiveness and love through the sacrificial atonement of Jesus Christ. Following this comes this command from Jesus: believe.

Repent. Receive. Believe.

Like gears in a car, these three steps will take you where you need to go. Whatever you face right now may be challenging. Like Naaman, it may even appear unsolvable. But if you will repent, receive, and believe today, God can do a work in your life like you've never imagined. He can turn things around and set you on the path of His greatest plan and purpose for your life. Will you trust Him? Will you believe? The choice is yours. We've seen as we've studied biblical accounts and scriptural stories that the choice for healing and restoration was up to each person we looked at. Similarly, the choice is now yours. You can see the sign: "U-turn available up ahead." Will you take it, and get back on the right path? It is my prayer that you do, and that when you do, you will witness the healing, restoring, and loving hand of Jesus Christ reversing consequences in your life.

APPENDIX

The Urban Alternative

The Urban Alternative (TUA) equips, empowers, and unites Christians to impact *individuals*, *families*, *churches*, and *communities* through a thoroughly kingdom agenda worldview. In teaching truth, we seek to transform lives.

The core cause of the problems we face in our personal lives, homes, churches, and societies is a spiritual one; therefore, the only way to address it is spiritually. We've tried a political, social, economic, and even a religious agenda.

It's time for a **kingdom agenda**.

The kingdom agenda can be defined as the visible manifestation of the comprehensive rule of God over every area of life.

The unifying central theme throughout the Bible is the glory of God and the advancement of His kingdom. The conjoining thread from Genesis to Revelation—from beginning to end—is focused on one thing: God's glory through advancing God's kingdom.

When you do not recognize that theme, the Bible becomes disconnected stories that are great for inspiration but seem to be unrelated in purpose and direction. Understanding the role of the kingdom in Scripture increases the relevancy of this several thousand-year-old text to your day-to-day living, because the kingdom is not only then, it is now.

The absence of the kingdom's influence in our personal lives, family lives, churches, and communities has led to a deterioration in our world of immense proportions:

- People live segmented, compartmentalized lives because they lack God's kingdom worldview.
- Families disintegrate because they exist for their own satisfaction rather than for the kingdom.
- Churches are limited in the scope of their impact because they fail to comprehend that the goal of the church is not the church itself, but the kingdom.
- Communities have nowhere to turn to find real solutions for real people who have real problems because the church has become divided, in-grown, and unable to transform the cultural landscape in any relevant way.

The kingdom agenda offers us a way to see and live life with a solid hope by optimizing the solutions of heaven. When God is no longer the final and authoritative standards under which all else falls, order and hope leaves with Him. But the reverse of that is true as well: as long as you have God, you have hope. If God is still in the picture, and as long as His agenda is still on the table, it's not over.

Even if relationships collapse, God will sustain you. Even if finances dwindle, God will keep you. Even if dreams die, God will revive you. As long as God, and His rule, is still the overarching standard in your life, family, church, and community, there is always hope.

Our world needs the King's agenda. Our churches need the King's agenda. Our families need the King's agenda.

We've put together a three-part plan to direct us to heal the divisions and strive for unity as we move toward the goal of truly being one nation under God. This three-part plan calls us to assemble with others in unity, address the issues that divide us, and to act together for social impact. Following this plan, we will see individuals, families, churches, and communities transformed as we follow God's kingdom agenda in every area of our lives. You can request this plan by sending an email to info@tonyevans.org or by going online to tonyevans.org.

In many major cities, there is a loop that drivers can take when they want to get somewhere on the other side of the city, but don't necessarily want to head straight through downtown. This loop will take you close enough to the city so that you can see its towering buildings and skyline, but not close enough to actually experience it.

This is precisely what we, as a culture, have done with God. We have put Him on the "loop" of our personal, family, church, and community lives. He's close enough to be at hand should we need Him in an emergency, but far enough away that He can't be the center of who we are.

We want God on the "loop," not the King of the Bible who comes downtown into the very heart of our ways. Leaving God on the "loop" brings about dire consequences as we have seen in our own lives and with others. But when we make God, and His rule, the centerpiece of all we think, do or say, it is then that we will experience Him in the way He longs for us to experience Him.

He wants us to be kingdom people with kingdom minds set on fulfilling His kingdom's purposes. He wants us to pray, as Jesus did, "Not My will, but Yours be done" (Luke 22:42 NASB). Because His is the kingdom, the power, and the glory (Matt. 6:13 NASB).

There is only one God, and we are not Him. As King and Creator, God calls the shots. It is only when we align ourselves underneath His comprehensive hand that we will access His full power and authority in all spheres of life: personal, familial, ecclesiastical, and societal.

As we learn how to govern ourselves under God, we then transform the institutions of family, church, and society from a biblically based kingdom worldview.

Under Him, we touch heaven and change the earth.

To achieve our goal, we use a variety of strategies, approaches, and resources for reaching and equipping as many people as possible.

Broadcast Media

Millions of individuals experience *The Alternative with Dr. Tony Evans* through the daily radio broadcast playing on nearly **1,400 radio outlets** and in more than **130 countries**. The broadcast can also be seen on several television networks and is available online at tonyevans.org. You can also listen to or view the daily broadcast by downloading the Tony Evans app for free in the App store. More than 30 million message downloads/streams occur each year.

Leadership Training

The Tony Evans Training Center (TETC) facilitates educational programming that embodies the ministry philosophy of Dr. Tony Evans as expressed through the kingdom agenda. The training courses focus on leadership development and discipleship in the following five tracks:

- Bible and Theology
- Personal Growth
- Family and Relationships
- Church Health and Leadership Development
- Society and Community Impact Strategies

The TETC program includes courses for both local and online students. Furthermore, TETC programming includes course work for nonstudent attendees. Pastors, Christian leaders, and Christian laity, both local and at a distance, can seek out The Kingdom Agenda Certificate for personal, spiritual, and professional development. For more information, visit: tonyevanstraining.org

The Kingdom Agenda Pastors (KAP) provides a *viable network* for *like-minded pastors* who embrace the kingdom-agenda philosophy. Pastors have the opportunity to go deeper with Dr. Tony Evans as they are given greater biblical knowledge, practical applications, and resources to impact individuals, families, churches, and communities. KAP welcomes *senior and associate pastors* of all churches. KAP also offers an annual Summit held each year in Dallas, with intensive seminars, workshops, and resources. For more information, visit: KAFellowship.org.

Pastors' Wives Ministry, founded by Dr. Lois Evans, provides *counsel, encouragement,* and *spiritual resources* for pastors' wives as they serve with their husbands in the ministry. A primary focus of the ministry is the KAP Summit that offers senior pastors' wives a safe place to *reflect, renew,* and *relax* along with training in personal development, spiritual growth, and care for their emotional and physical well-being. For more information, visit: LoisEvans.org.

Kingdom Community Impact

The outreach programs of The Urban Alternative seek to provide positive impact to individuals, churches, families, and communities through a variety of ministries. We see these efforts as necessary to our calling as a ministry and essential to the communities we serve. With training on how to initiate and maintain programs to adopt schools, or provide homeless services, or partner toward unity and justice with the local police precincts, which creates a connection between the police and our community, we, as a ministry, live out God's kingdom agenda according to our *Kingdom Strategy for Community Transformation*.

The *Kingdom Strategy for Community Transformation* is a three-part plan that equips churches to have a positive impact on their communities for the kingdom of God. It also provides numerous practical suggestions for how this three-part plan can be implemented in your community, and it serves as a blueprint for unifying churches around the common goal of creating a better world for all of us. For more information, visit: TonyEvans.org and click on the link to access the three-part plan.

National Church Adopt-a-School Initiative (NCAASI) prepares churches across the country to impact communities by using *public schools as the primary vehicle for effecting positive social change* in urban youth and families. Leaders of churches, school districts, faith-based organizations, and other nonprofit organizations are equipped with the knowledge and tools to *forge partnerships* and build *strong social service delivery systems*. This training is based on the comprehensive church-based community impact strategy conducted by Oak Cliff Bible Fellowship. It addresses such areas as economic development, education, housing, health revitalization, family renewal, and racial reconciliation. We assist churches in tailoring the model to meet specific needs of their communities while simultaneously addressing the spiritual and moral frame of reference. Training events are held annually in the Dallas area at Oak Cliff Bible Fellowship. For more information, visit: ChurchAdoptaSchool.org.

Athlete's Impact (AI) exists as an outreach both into and through the sports arena. Coaches can be the most influential factor in young people's lives, even ahead of their parents. With the growing rise of fatherlessness in our culture, more young people are looking to their coaches for guidance, character development, practical needs, and hope. After coaches on the influencer scale fall athletes. Athletes (whether professional or amateur) influence younger athletes and kids within their spheres of impact. Knowing this, we have made it our aim to equip and train coaches and athletes on how to live out and utilize their God-given roles for the benefit of the kingdom. We aim to do this through our iCoach App as well as resources such as *The Playbook: A Life Strategy Guide for Athletes.* For more information, visit: ICoachApp.org.

Tony Evans Films ushers in positive life change through compelling video shorts, animation, and feature-length films. We seek to build kingdom disciples through the power of story. We use a variety of platforms for viewer consumption and have more than 10 millon+ digital views. We also merge video-shorts and film with relevant Bible study materials to bring people to the saving knowledge of Jesus Christ and to strengthen the body of Christ worldwide. *Tony Evans Films* released its first feature-length film, *Kingdom Men Rising*, in April 2019 in over 800 theaters nationwide, in partnership with Lifeway Films. The second release, *Journey with Jesus*, is in partnership with RightNow Media.

Resource Development

We are fostering lifelong learning partnerships with the people we serve by providing a variety of published materials. Dr. Evans has published more than 125 unique titles based on more than fifty years of preaching, whether that is in booklet, book, or Bible study format. He also holds the honor of writing and publishing the first full-Bible commentary and study Bible by an African American, released in 2019. This Bible sits in permanent display as a historic release, in The Museum of the Bible in Washington, D.C.

For more information, and a complimentary copy of Dr. Evans' devotional newsletter, call (800) 800–3222 *or* write TUA at P.O. Box 4000, Dallas TX 75208, *or* visit us online at www.TonyEvans.org.

Notes

1. https://nonprofitssource.com/online-giving-statistics/, "The Ultimate List of Charitable Giving Statistics for 2018," accessed January 27, 2020.

2. https://abcnews.go.com/blogs/headlines/2014/02/heres-a-list-of-58-gender-options-for-facebook-users, "Here's a List of 58 Gender Options for Facebook Users" by Russell Goldman, February 13, 2014, accessed January 28, 2020.

Steps to Peace With God

1. God's Purpose: Peace and Life

God loves you and wants you to experience peace and life—abundant and eternal.

The Bible says ...

"We have peace with God through our Lord Jesus Christ." *Romans 5:1, NKJV*

"For God so loved the world that He gave His only begotten Son, that whoever believes in Him should not perish but have everlasting life." *John 3:16, NKJV*

"I have come that they may have life, and that they may have it more abundantly." *John 10:10, NKJV*

Since God planned for us to have peace and the abundant life right now, why are most people not having this experience?

2. Our Problem: Separation From God

God created us in His own image to have an abundant life. He did not make us as robots to automatically love and obey Him, but gave us a will and a freedom of choice.

We chose to disobey God and go our own willful way. We still make this choice today. This results in separation from God.

The Bible says ...

"For all have sinned and fall short of the glory of God." *Romans 3:23, NKJV*

"For the wages of sin is death, but the gift of God is eternal life in Christ Jesus our Lord." *Romans 6:23, NKJV*

Our choice results in separation from God.

People (Sinful)

God (Holy)

Our Attempts

Through the ages, individuals have tried in many ways to bridge this gap ... without success ...

The Bible says ...

"There is a way that seems right to a man, but its end is the way of death."
Proverbs 14:12, NKJV

"But your iniquities have separated you from your God; and your sins have hidden His face from you, so that He will not hear."
Isaiah 59:2, NKJV

There is only one remedy for this problem of separation.

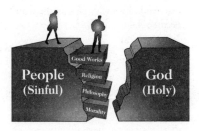

3. God's Remedy: The Cross

Jesus Christ is the only answer to this problem. He died on the cross and rose from the grave, paying the penalty for our sin and bridging the gap between God and people.

The Bible says ...

"For there is one God and one Mediator between God and men, the Man Christ Jesus."
1 Timothy 2:5, NKJV

"For Christ also suffered once for sins, the just for the unjust, that He might bring us to God."
1 Peter 3:18, NKJV

"But God shows his love for us in that while we were still sinners, Christ died for us." *Romans 5:8, ESV*

God has provided the only way ... we must make the choice ...

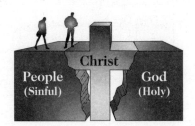

4. Our Response: Receive Christ

We must trust Jesus Christ and receive Him by personal invitation.

The Bible says ...

"Behold, I stand at the door and knock. If anyone hears My voice and opens the door, I will come in to him and dine with him, and he with Me." *Revelation 3:20, NKJV*

"But to all who did receive him, who believed in his name, he gave the right to become children of God." *John 1:12, ESV*

"If you confess with your mouth that Jesus is Lord and believe in your heart that God raised him from the dead, you will be saved." *Romans 10:9, ESV*

Are you here ... or here?

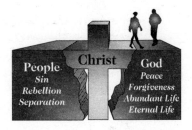

Is there any good reason why you cannot receive Jesus Christ right now?

How to Receive Christ:

1. Admit your need (say, "I am a sinner").
2. Be willing to turn from your sins (repent) and ask for God's forgiveness.
3. Believe that Jesus Christ died for you on the cross and rose from the grave.
4. Through prayer, invite Jesus Christ to come in and control your life through the Holy Spirit (receive Jesus as Lord and Savior).

What to Pray:

Dear God,
I know that I am a sinner. I want to turn from my sins, and I ask for Your forgiveness. I believe that Jesus Christ is Your Son. I believe He died for my sins and that You raised Him to life. I want Him to come into my heart and to take control of my life. I want to trust Jesus as my Savior and follow Him as my Lord from this day forward.

In Jesus' Name, amen.

_____   _____

Date   Signature

God's Assurance: His Word

If you prayed this prayer,

the Bible says ...

"For 'everyone who calls on the name of the Lord will be saved.'"
Romans 10:13, ESV

Did you sincerely ask Jesus Christ to come into your life? Where is He right now? What has He given you?

"For by grace you have been saved through faith. And this is not your own doing; it is the gift of God, not a result of works, so that no one may boast." *Ephesians 2:8–9, ESV*

the Bible says ...

"He who has the Son has life; he who does not have the Son of God does not have life. These things I have written to you who believe in the name of the Son of God, that you may know that you have eternal life, and that you may continue to believe in the name of the Son of God."
1 John 5:12–13, NKJV

Receiving Christ, we are born into God's family through the supernatural work of the Holy Spirit, who indwells every believer. This is called regeneration or the "new birth."

This is just the beginning of a wonderful new life in Christ. To deepen this relationship you should:

1. Read your Bible every day to know Christ better.
2. Talk to God in prayer every day.
3. Tell others about Christ.
4. Worship, fellowship, and serve with other Christians in a church where Christ is preached.
5. As Christ's representative in a needy world, demonstrate your new life by your love and concern for others.

God bless you as you do.

Franklin Graham

If you want further help in the decision you have made, write to:
Billy Graham Evangelistic Association
1 Billy Graham Parkway, Charlotte, NC 28201-0001

1-877-2GRAHAM (1-877-247-2426)
BillyGraham.org/commitment